SIT STILL

by

Leslie Sousa

SIT STILL

This is a work of fiction. All characters and events portrayed in this book belong to the author, and any resemblance to real people is purely coincidental.

For information contact: Sonflower Publishing Company at lesliesousa@live.com.

ISBN: 979-8-9861870-0-6

Cover design and Illustrations: Karen Borrelli
Editor: Rosalie Carlberg

PRINTED IN THE UNITED STATES OF

AMERICA

Dedication

When I was a kid, I loved nothing more than choosing one of the colored patterns from the oval, braided rug that sat under our dining room table and walking as fast as I could around it. I did all this while trying to stay on one pattern. It was my personal racetrack. I especially enjoyed doing this while my father sat at the table. Middle-aged with two grown sons of my own, I now know that I must have been driving him crazy. Often my father would say, "Can you just sit still and go light somewhere!" The expression light comes from an Irish blessing, "May the wings of the butterfly kiss the sun. And find your shoulder to light on."

This book is for my dad.

Keeping a fast pace didn't stop when I grew up. I used it as a defense mechanism repeatedly as an adult. When the tough times came, I got busy. Busyness kept me from thinking, feeling painful emotions, and the loneliness I associated with my childhood. If anyone asked about a situation, I could say, "Oh that, I've hardly given it a second thought." And it was a true statement.

Sit Still is a 52-week devotional, along with other encouraging stories, about what I discovered when I finally learned to "sit still" before the Lord. I invite you to pull up a chair and sit alongside me each week to begin a personal relationship with the Lord or deepen the one you already have.

Let your faith be deepened, your burdens lifted, your heart joyful, and your hope made new as you quiet yourself before the Lord, cease doing, and listen.

SIT STILL
A 52-week journey
with Leslie Sousa

Dedicated in loving memory of
Robert Lester Hilligoss
who always did the best he could

Part 1
God Seeking Man

For the Son of Man came to seek and to save the lost.
Luke 19:10

1
Listening to the Still Small Voice

Listen for God's voice in everything you do, everywhere you go; He's the One who will keep you on track. Proverbs 3:6 (online Bible Study Tools)

As I sat across the table from my husband one Friday date night, I told him I was ready to start writing a second book. I had already started writing one, but during the last couple of days, following weeks of prayer regarding what step I should take next, my idea for the book had changed entirely. My pastor had mentioned the importance of an excellent devotional book during one of his recent teachings. At that moment, I knew I would try to write one. I told my husband how my dad used to ask me if I could just sit still and go light somewhere and how I was going to use part of that phrase for the title. My husband suggested the oval, braided rug, and the empty chair on the cover. Loving that idea, I surprised myself when I told him that I would be dedicating this book to my dad. A decision I made when the words came out of my mouth.

Once they came out, I quickly and privately asked myself where the idea had come from, as my relationship with my dad had not always been an easy one for me. Writing a devotional and the book's title were confirmed two days later when I opened the current devotional I was reading, *Streams in the Desert* by L.B. Cowman. It read, "Their strength is to sit still." Isaiah 30:7

Ask yourself this week, "Are you ready to sit still and be strong in your commitment to spending time with the Lord?" As you prepare to spend time in this book next week, make a list of things that tend to get in your way of sitting still before the Lord. Next to each obstacle on your list, write how you can overcome it when it happens. If a new obstacle pops up along the way, add it and the solution to your list.

I encourage you to make your time with the Lord your number one priority. Try your hardest not to let anything come between you and the Lord during the special time you have set aside for Him.

2
Only One Life

"For to me, to live is Christ and to die is gain." (the Apostle Paul) Philippians 1:21

Hanging opposite the bathtub where I was bathed every night as a child hung a thoughtfully and purposely positioned plaque. The words on this plaque lived on in my memory long after childhood baths were over; "Only one life, 'twill soon be past. Only what's done for Christ will last."

Like the poem C.T. Studd penned, it was;

"Two little lines I heard one day,
Traveling along life's busy way;
Bringing conviction to my heart,
And from my mind would not depart."

It wasn't until after my father's death in 1991 and my mother's death in 2013 I realized just how fast our lives truly go by, and I became more curious about the writer of that poem.

On December 2, 1860, Charles Thomas (C.T.) Studd was born to a well-to-do English family. After his father gave his life to the Lord following a meeting with D.L. Moody, C.T. Studd came to know the Lord at the age of sixteen. C.T. Studd was a famous cricket player. Instead of pursuing the sport, he chose to serve as a missionary in China, pastor a church in India for seven years, and finish up his life establishing missionary stations in Africa. He died at the age of seventy. I love how he described his desire to be a missionary, "Some want to live within the sound of church or chapel bell; I want to run a rescue shop within a yard of hell."

C.T. Studd wrote over two hundred hymns and translated the New Testament into the Kingwana language. Although only two lines adorned our bathroom wall, his poem continues beautifully...

Only one life, yes only one,
Soon will its fleeting hours be done;
Then, in 'that day' my Lord to meet,
And stand before His Judgement seat;

Only one life, 'twill soon be past,
Only what's done for Christ will last.
Only one life, the still small voice,
Gently pleads for a *better choice*
Bidding me selfish aims to leave,
And to God's holy will to cleave;
Only one life, 'twill soon be past,
Only what's done for Christ will last.

Only one life, a few brief years,
Each with its burdens, hopes, and fears;
Each with its days I must fulfill,
Living for self or in His will;

Only one life, 'twill soon be past,
Only what's done for Christ will last.
When this bright world would tempt me sore,
When Satan would a victory score;

When self would seek to have its way,
Then help me Lord with joy to say;
Only one life, 'twill soon be past,
Only what's done for Christ will last.

Give me Father, a purpose deep,
In joy or sorrow Thy word to keep;
Faithful and true what e'er the strife,
Pleasing Thee in my daily life;

Only one life, 'twill soon be past,
Only what's done for Christ will last.
Oh let my love with fervor burn,
And from the world now let me turn;

Living for Thee, and Thee alone,
Bringing Thee pleasure on Thy throne;
Only one life, "twill soon be past,
Only what's done for Christ will last.

Only one life, yes only one,
Now let me say, "Thy will be done";
And when at last I'll hear the call,
I know I'll say "twas worth it all";

Only one life, 'twill soon be past,
Only what's done for Christ will last."
Only one life, 'twill soon be past,
Only what's done for Christ will last.

And when I am dying, how happy I'll be,
If the lamp of my life has been burned out for Thee.

Please pray this prayer along with me and mean it with all your heart.

Lord, let my heart's desire be the better choice. Help me to live for Your will and not my own self-will. Please give me a deep purpose and let the lamp of my life be burned out for Thee, in Jesus' name.

3
When I Was Eight

And now these three remain: faith, hope and love. But the greatest of these is love. 1 Corinthians 13:13

The first clear memory I have of reading the Bible is at age eight. It was summer vacation and my mom, Alberta, read the Bible to my sister and me from 8:00 a.m. to 8:30 a.m. every day. Afterward, we were allowed to watch an episode of "I Love Lucy." My mom never watched the show with us because, as she explained it, Lucy made her extremely nervous.

My mom knew, no matter what Lucy was up to, she would get caught before the show was over. The anticipation of her getting caught was enough to make my mom find clothes to fold or dishes to do instead of watching with us.

I remember reading a lot of strange names in the Bible those thirty minutes, funny looks from my sister, and giggles that almost got us in trouble. But I also remember my mom's dedication to that time. I'd often see her outside later in the day, sitting in the sun with her sweater on. She'd have a mason jar full of iced water by her side, and she'd be reading that same Bible. She couldn't seem to get enough of it. I found it both curious and odd.

I am in my fifties now, and the other day this memory of my mother flashed across my mind. It may have been because I was sitting outside in the sun reading my Bible with a green tea from a local coffee shop. I had been sitting outside for the last three afternoons, reading and praying about this very book.

Don't ever think what you do doesn't impact those around you. Long after you are gone, the love you've shown, the encouragement you've given, and what you've made a priority in your life live on. It may be in a child, a relative, or the clerk at your local grocery store. Your love for the Lord, or lack of love, leaves a legacy.

We learn from 1 Corinthians 13:13 that love is the greatest of the three (faith, hope, and love). Are you showing "the greatest" to those around you and those watching you?"

How do you want to be remembered?

Ask yourself this week, "What kind of legacy am I leaving?" "Am I having the kind of impact on others that I want to have while I am alive?" Why or why not?

If you aren't having the kind of impact you would like to have, ask the Lord to use every ounce of you for His righteousness. My pastor says this is one prayer He will always answer.

4
My mom, Alberta

For where your treasure is, there your heart will be also. Matthew 6:21

Alberta loved a pot of black coffee
Getting up before dawn
Sitting in the sunshine
With her sweater on.

She loved camping
Hiking to the end of the trail
Her best friend, Rita
Getting cards in the mail.

She loved her neighbors
Baking all kinds of treats
For my childhood friends
At each end of the street.

She loved sharing zucchini
Fresh from her garden
Opening her door
To all those downtrodden.

She loved coffee candy
See's candy too
And if you didn't like yours
She'd gladly eat it for you.

She loved sewing doll dresses
Sugared orange peels
A little bite of dessert
After each meal.

She loved reading her Bible
Exercising to Jack LaLanne
Walking with her pink umbrella
Out in the rain.

She loved baking with me
Bonbons each year
The mountains, the pine trees
But mostly the deer.

She loved a big glass of iced water
Collecting porcelain dolls
The color of turquoise
And every phone call.

She loved taking prayer requests
Lending an ear
Being a friend
To those far and near.

She loved playing country gospel music
Singing out loud
Watching the 4th of July parade
Holding her flag proud.

She loved playing the piano
In the senior citizen band
Walking the pier in Santa Cruz
Bread to feed the birds in hand.

She loved the rollercoaster
She'd ride it many times
The second she'd get off
You could find her back in line.

She loved going to church
The more services, the better
Being independent and free
She loved writing and letters.

She loved her Bible study
A group together forty years
She loved everyone's casserole
Sharing good cheer.

She loved hamburgers for breakfast
Grilled onions too
And if you ever met her
I know she would love you!

She loved many things
But only one beyond measure
Time spent in the Bible with the Savior
Was her greatest treasure.

Ask yourself this week, "Where is my treasure?" Is that where you want your heart to be also? If not, ask God to change your heart, and He will.

5
Nine

For we live by faith, not by sight. 2 Corinthians 5:7

When I was nine, my teacher sternly told our class of 3rd graders that, under no circumstances were we allowed to get up or ask any questions during the test. I was a very respectful and conscientious student, so I kept quiet when the teacher began to write the questions on the blackboard at the front of the room, and I could not see them from the back. When she finished writing the questions, the classroom was silent as the other students did as they were told and started taking the test. My mind was anything but calm. I was filled with fear. I was going to fail the test.

I raised my hand. "Leslie," she said in the same stern, instructive voice, "There will be no questions until after the test." I put my hand down as I could feel my heart pounding in my chest.

I stood up. This behavior was so unlike me that I couldn't understand why the teacher wouldn't give me a chance to explain. I had never gone against her wishes, talked back, or been in the least bit disrespectful. She told me to sit back down, and I did.

As my eyes welled up with tears, I could no longer hold them in. They came out in the loudest sob I had ever heard, and by the looks of the other children, the loudest sob they had ever heard too! My teacher rushed over, took me to the back of the room, and asked me kindly, "Leslie, what's wrong?" I could barely breathe by this point, as I told her that I couldn't see the board, that I couldn't take the test, and that I was going to fail.

She told me she would move me to the front row, and that's all it took. I stopped crying and sat down where she led me. I could hear the other kid's snide remarks as I took the test, but I didn't care. I could see the questions, and I knew the answers.

Shortly after this, I was given an appointment with the school nurse, and she tested my eyes. I wore thick glasses from then on, but this would not be the end of my eye issues.

My mom used to order these little books by the box called tracks. I remember her handing them out proudly to the people she'd meet. Occasionally, she'd leave one on the table for our server after eating out. One of the tracks was even called *Here's a Tip*.

The one, my mom, grabbed from her purse at this moment was called *Teach Us to Pray.* She read through it from the car as she watched my dad pace the sidewalk outside the waiting room at the optometrist's office. When he crossed the street, she could see the worry on his face as he told her my eyes were deteriorating at the rate of an older adult, and there was a good chance I would go blind. The optometrist referred me to a specialist and tried to get me in to see him as soon as possible. My mom started crying and praying as she later described in a poem she wrote:

Eyes to See

Please don't let this be,
Unless through her blindness,
You somehow get the glory.

When we see the specialist, and he examines
Leslie's eyes,
Let all the deterioration have disappeared.
Let him be surprised.

The little book, "Teach Us to Pray," was stained with tears as my mom put it back in her purse.

It was getting close to Easter, and my sister and brother were away on choir tour with a local church, so my parents gathered me up in their arms and took me to the store.

In my book, *Let the Son Shine In*, I answered my mom's poem with one of my own:

My Eyes to See

Standing in the aisle
I looked into your eyes
The tear upon your cheek
Caught me by surprise

I could feel your sadness
As I heard you say
Choose as much candy as you want, dear
It will soon be Easter day.

I chose a chocolate bunny
In a pink foil dress
A blue one for my sister
For my brother, the biggest and the best.

The candy seemed sky high
Many choices I could make
But I didn't care about more candy
I only thought of your heartache.

I took your hand in mine
I whispered in your ear,
"Why are you so sad, mommy?"
As your eyes welled up with tears.

I knew for me you cried
Yet I was not afraid
For I was just a child
And you the one so brave.

I don't remember Easter
Or much about that day
But I do remember your quiet sobs
When we heard the doctor say,

"You will see the flowers,
The quiet sunsets and sunrise,
The birds and God's creation,
With your beautiful blue eyes."

I watched you, and I learned
To thank God with all my might
But the deeper lesson that you taught me was
To walk by faith and not by sight.

I found out much later
Something else about that day
My dad stood against our back fence
Bowed his head and he prayed,

"God, please don't let Leslie
Ever go blind.
Instead of her eyes Lord,
You can take mine."

Through this heartache, my mom learned to trust God to bring her through every situation. Her faith is captured at the end of her poem:

The darkest days that life can bring,
I'll trust Him now with everything.

I never sang my favorite childhood song, "We Walk by Faith, Not by Sight" by Marj Snyder, the same way again.

It is incredible how God uses the darkest days that life can bring to draw us closer to Him.

Are you in a dark place this week? If so, I encourage you to give whatever is troubling you over to The One who crawls into the darkness with you. Ask Him to be your light in the dark, and He will.

6
The Baseball Game

Therefore do not worry about tomorrow, for tomorrow will worry about itself. Each day has enough trouble of its own. Matthew 6:34

It was pitch black outside. I knew I should have been fast asleep by now, but thoughts of tomorrow were keeping me awake. As I lay in my bed, I thought about how I would know if our team had won the championship baseball game or not by this time the next day.

The game would be during the lunch hour at my elementary school. I was excited, but I was also nervous. Although I was quite a tomboy at age eleven, I wasn't the best player. But what I lacked in skill, I made up in enthusiasm. I knew I had given those games my all as I asked the Lord quietly from covers pulled up tightly to my chin, "Will you please help my team win the game tomorrow?" With that and eyes I could no longer hold open, I gave the game to God and went to sleep.

The bell signaling the end of our lunch break would go off at any second, and my team was ahead by one point. The other team was up, had two outs, and bases were loaded. Tensions were high as I stood in the outfield.

When the batter took a hard swing and hit the ball, it flew high into the air. When I looked up, the ball was coming right at me! I couldn't believe it!

Not only did we win the championship game that day, but I also caught the fly ball that was responsible for the win, and all within a second of the bell ringing.

It is wonderful to know that God cares about the little things that strengthen our faith. We may not win every championship game, but God promises to bend down His ear and listen intently when we pray to Him with the faith of a child. I can only imagine what a delight it must have been for Him to answer my earnest prayer the way that He did and the joy it brought Him when I prayed a prayer of thanksgiving that night, giving Him all the credit.

Are thoughts of tomorrow, next week, or next year keeping you awake? I know we can't compare our adult problems to a child's championship game, but coming before the Lord humbly with complete dependence and casting our cares on Him like a child can make all the difference.

The Bible says in Matthew 18:2-4, "He called a little child to him, and placed the child among them. And he said: "Truly I tell you, unless you change and become like little children, you will never enter the kingdom of heaven. Therefore, whoever takes the lowly position of this child is the greatest in the kingdom of heaven."

I encourage you to give whatever keeps you awake at night to The One who never sleeps.

I'd like you to memorize the following verse with me and meditate on it this week.

When you lie down, you will not be afraid; when you lie down, your sleep will be sweet. Proverbs 3:24

Now personalize it and thank Him for the gift of sleep.

When I lie down, I will not be afraid; when I lie down, my sleep will be sweet. Thank you, Father, for the gift of sweet sleep, knowing that when I lay down, I can truly rest in You.

7
Twelve

All those the Father gives me will come to me, and whoever comes to me I will never send away. John 6:37

I stood alone in a downtown church during an altar call when I was twelve. A neighbor had picked me up and taken me to church, but for now, I stood alone. I remember the song they were singing, "Just as I Am."

Charlotte Elliott wrote these lyrics in 1835:

Just as I am, without one plea
But that Thy blood was shed for me
And that Thou bid'st me come to Thee
O Lamb of God, I come! I come

Just as I am, though tossed about
With many a conflict, many a doubt
Fighting and fears within without
O Lamb of God, I come, I come

Just as I am, and waiting not
To rid my soul of one dark blot
To thee whose blood can cleanse each spot
O Lamb of God, I come, I come

I clearly remember the tugging on my heart as I started singing along and the still small voice that called me to step out and walk down the aisle. It was scary, but at the same time, I felt a boldness. I had asked Jesus into my heart when I was eight years old, but today was different. I could hear the still small voice of the Holy Spirit calling me.

If there is stillness in your heart, you will be able to hear God's whisper there.

"After the earthquake came a fire, but the Lord was not in the fire. And after the fire came a gentle whisper." 1 Kings 19:12

Have you ever felt a tug on your heart? Will you answer His call to come if you haven't done so already? If you've never asked Him into your heart, I encourage you to step out in faith and make Him the priority of your life, not this week, but today.

Just as I am, poor, wretched, blind
Sight, riches, healing of the mind
Yea, all I need, in Thee to find
O Lamb of God, I come, I come!

Just as I am, Thou wilt receive
Wilt welcome, pardon, cleanse, relieve
Because Thy promise I believe
O Lamb of God, I come, I come.

If you are already a Christian, ask yourself, "Has God given me another call on my life that I can answer this week?"

8
Come To Me

For God so loved the world that He gave His one and only Son, that whoever believes in Him shall not perish but have eternal life. John 3:16

Charles Stanley is the founder of In Touch Ministries and Pastor Emeritus of First Baptist Church of Atlanta, Georgia, where he served more than 50 years. He encourages his listeners to write this definition down and to share it with others:

"*To believe in Jesus* is to have a confident conviction that He is who the Bible says He is, He will keep His promises, and upon placing your trust in Him, you are entering into a personal, eternal relationship with the Son of God."

Do you believe it?

I need to ask you the most important question of your life. Your very life and afterlife depend on the answer. Have you placed your trust in Jesus Christ? If you have, congratulations! If not, is He calling you to begin a relationship with Him today?

"Behold, I stand at the door and knock. If anyone hears My voice and opens the door, I will come in..." Revelation 3:20

If your answer is yes, all you have to do is pray this prayer and mean it with your whole heart:

Dear God, as You stand at the door and knock, I open my heart to You. I realize I am less than perfect (a sinner). I ask You to forgive me of my sins. I believe You sent Your only Son to die in my place for my sins. Make me who I am supposed to be in Jesus Christ. I thank You for coming into my life and for saving me. In Jesus' name. Amen.

If you have prayed this prayer this week, tell somebody.

I encourage you to write or sign and date your name on the next page.

If you have already given your life to Jesus Christ, share this devotion with someone else this week.

BOOK OF LIFE

On______________________________
Today's date

____
Name

Gave his/her life to Christ!

9
After the Tug on my Heart

You will lead me in the path of life. I experience absolute joy in your presence; you always give me sheer delight. Psalm 16:11

After going forward at church and praying privately with a very kind lady to re-dedicate my life to the Lord, I asked to be baptized in the name of the Father, the Son, and the Holy Spirit. Three months later, I was baptized by being immersed in water.

Later that year, as it was getting close to summer vacation, I was asked to teach the Bible to the children of the women who attended the same Bible study as my mother. In my mind, I was "grown-up," and they were much younger than I was. But in truth, some of the age difference was only a few years.

I was excited to be asked. I felt I had been tasked with something significant. I remember sitting down with my Bible time and time again that summer, putting together lessons for my own Bible study group. It was the best summer I ever had! I was joyful! The Bible study was important to me. The children were important to me too, and I wanted them to learn something. I grew to love this time with the Lord. Something about spending time with Him made me happier than I had ever been. So much so that I have never forgotten the peace that welled up inside of me that summer. That's what spending time with the Lord does.

Ask yourself today and in this coming week, "Am I happy?" "Am I experiencing God's joy?" I promise you can find both in spending time with the Lord.

When my mom died in 2013, her Bible study group had met weekly for over forty years!

10
The Most Painful Emotion

But this is to fulfill what is written in their Law: 'They hated me without reason.' John 15:25

Going to high school church camp was an exciting time for me. I was looking forward to being independent and seeing what the week ahead would hold.

When our bus arrived, I was anxious to unload my backpack onto one of the six bunk beds in a small cabin designated for the girls. I looked around at the other girls who were picking out their bunks. I'd seen them before, but I didn't know any of them. I wasn't bothered by that, though.

I knew soon we'd all be laughing and getting acquainted. I took in all the beauty of the surrounding mountains from a small window. "A whole week!" I thought as one of the staff members called us to dinner.

I enjoyed most of the camp; the Bible studies, walks, quiet time, food, and games, but many of the girls weren't very friendly towards me. There hadn't been any laughs in the cabin, at least not ones that included me. When I went into the dressing area, where most of the girls were French braiding each other's hair and asked for someone to put my hair in French braids, I was mostly frowned upon. "Was this my imagination?" I wondered, "Wasn't this church where everyone was supposed to be accepted?"

On the last night of camp, I was ready to go home. As we sat in a lovely, solid wood sanctuary for the final teaching, the pastor went in a direction I wasn't expecting. "Have you hurt anyone this week?" he asked, "Have you talked behind anyone's back? Do you need to ask that person for forgiveness before you go home?" I felt no nudging in my spirit as I half-listened and wrote poetry in the notebook meant for my Bible notes. But I couldn't help noticing the line forming in front of me. I was shocked! One by one, they apologized to me. I wondered if the line would ever end.

I have known the sting of rejection many times over the years. From the mean girls at church to the uncertainty of my father's love for me growing up. From the abandonment of a partner I had pledged my life to, to friends I dearly loved who couldn't be there for me for one reason or another. Rejection hurts… terribly. I honestly believe rejection is one of the most painful emotions there is. But nothing compares to the rejection our Savior endured on our behalf.

Have you ever been the last kid chosen for the team? Have you ever sat in the school cafeteria alone? When it seems like no one else sees you, God sees you. You are loved, and you matter.

If someone you've loved has tossed you aside, you are not alone. There is someone here for you who is greater than any hurt you have experienced. It is the almighty God who promises never to abandon you. Take hold of this great promise and ask Him to heal your wounded heart. He wants to, He can, and He will.

Find a group or a church this week where you can meet other like-minded people because God doesn't want you to be alone either.

11
Fred

I do not hide your righteousness in my heart; I speak of your faithfulness and your saving help. I do not conceal your love and your faithfulness from the great assembly. Psalm 40:10

I was barely eighteen
Out looking for work
When I found a job
As a medical records clerk.

I worked Monday through Friday
From eight to five
My dad dropped me off
I had no car to drive.

Sometimes during lunch
I would wander the hall
Hear the clanking of trays
The elderly call.

On this particular day
Outside room 203
Was a well-dressed gentleman
Who was looking at me.

"Excuse me," he said
"But would you mind
Pushing me down
To the place where we dine?"

I looked at my watch
With ten minutes to spare
I was sure I had time
To get him down there.

I turned his wheelchair around
Headed for the hall
"My name is Fred," he said
"Tomorrow, we go to the mall."

I had heard of this trip
Seen a flyer on the board
But I couldn't really understand
What Fred was looking towards.

Pushed up to the table
I watched him get his tray
I smiled, and I waved
As I walked away.

Back in the office
Two hours flew by
When I noticed a familiar face
Out of the corner of my eye.

Tap-tap on the front glass
I caught a glimpse of his hand
I opened the office window
To find something unplanned.

It was Fred; he'd come to see me
He wanted to know
If to the mall tomorrow
I wanted to go!

My boss stood behind me
Overhearing his request
"I don't need you,"
He politely confessed.

The next morning by the bus
I was happy to find
It was to Fred for the day
I had been assigned.

They gave us instructions
Like where to meet at
I looked at Fred fondly
My new friend in the hat.

When we got on the bus
The group was so small
Didn't look like too many residents
Wanted to go to the mall.

Fred and I talked over lunch
We went in every store
I saw the mall
Like never before.

As Fred explained it to me
It was a way
To get out, to be free again
To keep old age at bay.

My adoration grew
As I listened to him
Talk of days gone by
Looking out from under his hat's brim.

It was a great day!
My best at the mall
Every day after
I pushed him to the dining hall.

I see Fred's life differently
Now that I'm older
I see the convalescent hospital
A little bit colder.

But more so for Fred, I wish I'd been bolder.

I never asked Fred
Do you know Jesus
If he wanted to pray
Or know Who really frees us?

I can only hope
When I get to Heaven
He'll be there, and so will the lady
From room 211.

Is there a time in your life you wish you'd been bolder? If there is, and you can still make it right, ask God to show you how to do that this week.

If it's too late to make the situation right, ask God for forgiveness. Ask Him to give you the strength you need to be bold for His name's sake in the future opportunities He will provide you with. Thank Him for using other people to touch those lives you failed to touch. Thank Him for bringing more of these opportunities into your life.

Ask God to bring to your remembrance anyone who needs you to share His love with them. Once you know who the person is, ask God how to share His love with that person this week.

Write down what the Lord led you to do and the person's reaction.

12
He Is with Us

The Lord himself goes before you and will be with you; he will never leave you nor forsake you. Do not be afraid; do not be discouraged. Deuteronomy 31:8

"It's not over 'til it's over," my boss said upon learning that my husband had just left me for the second time. She proceeded to hand me a book. It was a hardback, and it looked outdated. I thanked her, flipped through the "thou arts," and quickly put it in my dresser drawer when I got home.

A failed reconciliation, and two years later, I was living alone again and laying in my bed directly across from my dresser. I couldn't sleep. I was heartbroken, lonely, and scared. How was I going to pay the house payment, work full-time, and take care of all the needs of two little boys by myself? I sat up in bed and looked for something, anything, in my nightstand that I could read to take my mind off my current situation. Suddenly I remembered the book my boss had given me. Was it still in my dresser?

I got up, dug through a dresser drawer or two, and there it was, still looking old but much more inviting. Crawling back into bed, and after reading just the first page, I was hooked. I couldn't believe the treasure I had kept locked away. Francis Roberts had written it beautifully as if God were speaking directly to me, His one and only. The title was so fitting, *Come Away My Beloved.* I quickly felt a sense of peace envelope me as I read the second page and fell fast asleep. Reading this book became a nightly ritual until I had read the book thoroughly, from beginning to end, several times.

This book became my companion when I had to go to court over the next four years. I would read it as I waited for the courtroom deputy to call my case, and it never failed to bring me comfort. When I attended a DivorceCare support group, we sat in small groups around big tables. I gave each lady who sat at my table a copy of the book. They all loved it!

Think about the presence of God in your life this week. His very existence is awe-inspiring and overwhelmingly good. Do not be afraid if you are going through a trial of your own right now. He goes before you, and He will be with you through this trial and any that follow. He not only walks beside us, but He carries us when we need Him to. Ask Him to direct your steps and to speak to you through His Word in your present situation. He might even make sure you have some encouragement in your dresser drawer when you need it.

13
What If?

Then the Spirit said to Philip, 'Go up and join this chariot," Acts 8:29

$358.00 is precisely the amount He had told me to give her. I had grown very entuned to the Holy Spirit's promptings by this time. So, when I was preparing to see my hairstylist later that day, I wrote a check for $358.00 and put it in my pocket. Most of the times before, I had not seen the significance of what the Holy Spirit had led me to do. I wasn't surprised when I had no idea why the amount given to me was so specific.

After my usual shampoo, cut, and blow-dry, I felt nervous about handing her the check. A million "what ifs" filled my mind. What if I hadn't heard The Holy Spirit correctly? What if I didn't hear Him at all, and it's just my crazy idea? What if it isn't the right amount, or she thinks I'm weird? It's interesting how easily we can talk ourselves out of a Holy Spirit prompting.

But desiring to communicate the love of Christ to others by whatever means He tells me, I put those and a million other thoughts aside and stepped out in faith. I handed her the envelope. I told her how I had felt led to give her this exact amount. She gasped when she opened it.

Then she cried. It was the exact amount she needed to pay her car payment that month, and she could not believe it. Neither could I, really, but I have never forgotten how God used me.

I may not have gotten it right every time, but the only times I had regret were the times I talked myself out of following the promptings of the Holy Spirit. If I am unsure, I ask myself, "Is what I will do out of love?" "Will it encourage the person?" Sometimes I never know if, or how, something the Holy Spirit has led me to do has touched someone's life, but when I do know, there is nothing like it. There is an insurmountable joy in giving our time, love, and resources to others. Knowing God has used you to bless another person is one of the greatest blessings.

The Holy Spirit tunes us into the Father's voice and, in faith, we do what we believe He is calling us to do. Ask the Holy Spirit to tune you into the Father's voice each day this week, and ask Him to empower you to go where He leads.

14
Glowing

Look to the Lord and his strength; seek His face always. 1 Chronicles 16:11

I've heard it said that divorce is worse than death because it is a choice. I have experienced both, each with their unique pain, and I believe rejection to be the most painful.

In the fall of 1997, sitting next to me on a couch placed in the parlor of a home built in the early 1900s in a quaint little town in America, he told me he didn't love me anymore—his words heart- wrenching. The following day, I watched from an upstairs window as he carried a small box out to his car and drove away.

Three days later, I had the excruciating task of answering my son's question, "Where is daddy?" The memory of his little pained face and his response, "I don't understand. My dad and I had so much fun together," when I told him daddy was not going to live here anymore, still makes my heart drop at the thought of it some 20-plus years later.

Determined to be that one secure, stable parent the court had told me was all my boys needed to be okay, I went to the one place I have always gone to find victory. I went to the feet of my Savior. I was emotionally, physically, and mentally exhausted. I lived 40 minutes away from my job. I remember going into work the first day after "that day." I spent most of the day on the office couch, not wanting to go home to the emptiness. A bowl of soup was delivered to me by a co-worker at lunchtime.

I started making the most of the 40-minute commute by playing Christian sermons on tape on my way to work. They gave me the strength I needed to make it to lunchtime. I could only take life minute by minute, but that was okay because I started learning that what I did with those minutes was making all the difference.

When it was time for lunch, I would go to a nearby park and force myself to eat a few bites of something while reading a little book called "My Daily Bread." It's a small devotional that comes out every three months. You can order it at 616-974- 2210 or from odb@odb.org for free.

The hope I found in the devotional helped me hold on for the next few hours until it was time to clock out. I had time for another 40 minutes of Christian teachings on tape back in the car. I would pick up my kids from daycare, make dinner, help my oldest son with his elementary school homework, and put my youngest to bed. Having an easy baby who slept through the night was a blessing.

My oldest son and I would play Mrs. Potato Head because they were all out of Mr. Potato Head. Sometimes I would turn a cartoon on the tiny 24-inch T.V. set at the end of my bed for him to watch. Either way, I would fall asleep listening to my pastor's teachings on those same cassette tapes. I fed myself with God's Word, His truth, and His promises every chance I got.

Back at work, I was surprised to hear comments like, "You look great! Did you and your husband get back together?" We hadn't, and going to court became my new normal for the next four years. I was still that same hurting, scared, estranged wife, but something had indeed changed within me, and they could all see it. Some of my co-workers even said I looked like I glowed. I was finding strength at the feet of my Savior.

No matter how bad your heart is breaking, seek the Lord. If your heart is not breaking today, seek Him anyway. Feed your mind with His Word and His promises each morning, afternoon, and evening. Walk with Him. Talk with Him. Fill yourself up with His love, and He will give you His peace that surpasses all understanding. Time spent with your Savior is never wasted. It will never return void. This holds true whether the sermons are playing on cassette, CD, or Bluetooth. Times change. God does not!

As God takes you through trials, remember His faithfulness to you in the last one. Your faith in Him will grow as you see that you can count on Him, that He is reliable. He is life's only constant. He is the same yesterday, today, as He will be tomorrow, and you can trust Him.

Think about the trials you have been through and recall how God has helped you. Did you invite Him to walk alongside you through the trial, or were you not yet a Christian and felt helpless and alone?

Make a list this week of how you will approach subsequent trials. Ask yourself, how does He show His consistency in my life now?

15
The Lion

Then children were brought to him that he might lay his hands on them and pray. The disciples rebuked them, but Jesus said, "Let the children come to me, and do not prevent them; for the kingdom of heaven belongs to such as these." After he placed his hands on them, he went away. Matthew 19:13-15

My oldest son must have been all of 2 years old when I picked him up from the sitter that day. I had barely turned my car off when a little buddy of his came running, followed by the sitter. As I got out of my car and walked over to the sitter to ask about the day, my son's buddy persistently pulled on the hem of my dress. He had something important to say, and he wasn't giving up! I looked down at him to let him know he had my full attention. "He's lying! He's lying!" he said adamantly, pointing to my son as he ran towards me, arms stretched out wide. I lifted that little boy of mine, admiring his innocence. "Yes, mommy," he said, "I am a lion. Roooaaaarrrr!!!"

The innocence of a child is a beautiful treasure. God wants us to have this same innocence by being honest, unassuming, forgiving, and loving. Jesus wants us to rely on Him and follow His example as children do their parents.

Meditate on Mark 10:13-16 and Luke 18:15-17.

These verses tell us a lot about who Jesus was on the earth and how we should live our lives. It's incredible how comfortable children were with Jesus. There was no fear in them. When the Bible tells us to fear the Lord, it means to be in awe of Him and reverence Him, not to be afraid of Him.

What does God bring to your attention from the verses you just read?

Do you fear God in the right way? Do you try to follow His example by being loving and forgiving? Is there someone you need to forgive this week? If so, ask the Lord to help you find forgiveness in your heart for that person.

I know it's not easy. A few people in my life have deeply hurt me, and I have had a hard time forgiving them. My hardened heart didn't think they deserved forgiveness, but then I had to remind myself, neither do we deserve God's forgiveness. I started by simply asking God to bless the person who had offended me. Even this little request for them was hard for me at first. As I continued to ask the Lord to bless them, my prayers slowly got longer until God released me from the power my unforgiving spirit had over me.

Nothing good can come out of carrying around a spirit of unforgiveness. I've heard it said, "Unforgiveness is like drinking poison and waiting for the other person to die."

Ask God to help you let go of any bitterness this week that has held you captive, even if it just starts with a "bless, inserting the person's name." Let the healing begin. It's time.

16
The Gift of Spiritual Discernment

To another miraculous powers, to another prophecy, to another distinguishing spirits, to another speaking in different kinds of tongues, and to still another the interpretation of tongues. 1 Corinthians 12:10

He had called me at work several times. He had even interrupted me in an important meeting. No matter how many times I told him I didn't feel comfortable giving him the money, he kept asking. He said his parents needed it. When I got home from work, he was parked in front of my house. He said he would pay me back by the end of the night, but even that promise didn't shake the check in my spirit. I reminded him that times were tough, and now that I was a single mom, I couldn't lend him all of my savings. He finally left.

I was busy with my children throughout the evening. Still, as the night approached, I started second-guessing my decision not to help him. Maybe the money was for what he had said it was. Perhaps he would pay me back by the end of the night.

As these questions swirled in my mind, I took my toothbrush out to get ready for bed. I remember it as if it were yesterday. The voice wasn't audible, but I could hear it loud and clear! "The money is for…." and the real reason he had asked me for the money was revealed to me. That reason had never crossed my mind. In an attempt to verify the reason, I called a friend of his. This person would know, and they would tell me the truth. I was sure of that.

When I called his friend and asked the awkward question, there was no hesitation in his voice. "Yes," he said, "that's what the money is for." I could tell by the way he answered he thought I already knew. I said goodbye and hung up the phone.

Although it hurt to know the truth, I was thankful for the Holy Spirit's full disclosure. This revelation of the Holy Spirit gave me peace. It was a pivotal moment in my life, as I learned the importance of walking closely with the Lord, the extreme importance of listening, and the reliability of what He says to me.

He speaks to us through His Word, through prayer, through the Holy Spirit, and through trusted advisors and gifted teachers whose source is the Bible. He also speaks to us through past experiences, a sense of peace, by opening and closing doors, and through creation.

Read 1 Kings 18:20-40; 19:12, where God speaks to Elijah in a gentle whisper and ask God to help you hear what He wants to say to you this week.

Unconfessed sin, a wrong attitude, or resentment can create distance between our Savior and us. Ask God to help you recall anything you might need to ask forgiveness for. Restore the relationship with your very Best Friend and keep the lines of communication open.

When is the last time you sat quietly before the Lord in anticipation of hearing from Him? How can you make this a part of your daily devotions? Keep track of how God speaks to you as you sit quietly before Him each day this week.

17
The Note Word for Word

Come to me, all you who are weary and burdened, and I will give you rest. Take my yoke upon you and learn from me, for I am gentle and humble in heart, and you will find rest for your souls. For my yoke is easy, and my burden is light. Matthew 11:28-30

Dear Leslie,

"Greater things are going on than what meets the eye. Keep your focus upon Me," says the Lord, "and I will build upon your foundation what needs to be there. I know your heart and desire, and this is what you want. Praise Me in everything, even when you don't feel like it. Praise Me because I am faithful. Don't worry about your children. You have prayed and given them to Me. Now trust and relax. I will lead them and guide them. Stay focused upon Me and the big picture, which is saving lives."

This note still sits on my desk twelve years after a home Bible study leader gave it to me. The weight of worrying about tomorrow suddenly lifted when I read what she had written in the middle of the night with the words God had placed on her heart for me, His child. What comfort they brought then and still bring. I share this note in hopes that it will also encourage you. Below is how you can apply the message to your own life.

There is always more going on than what meets the human eye. If we keep our focus on the all-knowing

God, He will build upon the foundation He laid for us when we accepted Him as our Lord and Savior. He alone makes up for all that we lack, and it is He who keeps our foundation strong.

Let Him draw you to Himself. Sometimes that comes through pain. Once we understand that all He allows us to go through is for our good, we can sincerely start thanking Him through the storm.

A relationship with Him is the only thing that can fill the Christ-shaped hole in our hearts, and we all have one. You can try to fill it with food, shopping, work, and romantic relationships, but nothing will work. Many of you have already tried. Christ alone fills our hearts. He alone has the power to make us whole.

Praise Him when you feel like it and even more when you don't. Praise invites the fullness of God's presence and joy into our lives. Remember how Moses's face glowed after being in God's presence? Your face can too.

God is faithful. We don't have to worry about anything once we have given it to God. With abandoned surrender, make your requests known to God in prayer. As we draw closer to Him in the relationship and learn to abide in Him, we can trust and relax. He leads. He guides. He does all the work. Your job is to yield to His perfect will.

We are all called as Christians to the great commission, which is saving lives. Looking at the bigger picture helps us to keep things in perspective.

Go back to the beginning of the note and reread it, only insert your name in it this time. Are you weary and burdened? What specific burdens are you carrying this week? If kids aren't a concern currently, substitute and surrender whatever is once and for all. If you start to take what you have surrendered to God back under your control, surrender it to Him as many times as you need to.

Sometimes the process of surrendering can take time and practice, but He desires to carry your burdens and mine.

18
Jesus

He called a little child to him, and placed the child among them. And he said: "Truly I tell you, unless you change and become like little children, you will never enter the kingdom of heaven. Therefore, whoever takes the lowly position of this child is the greatest in the kingdom of heaven. Matthew 18:2-4

It was important that I take my two boys on a family vacation every summer. The vacations were nothing extravagant, but there was always at least a week's vacation to look forward to. I wanted them to have a fun, family memory along with an answer to the question, "What did you do this summer?" when they went back to school in September.

This year, it was a trip to Las Vegas. We planned to see the Blue Man Group and eat dinner without utensils (which they thought was great) alongside the Knights of the Round Table at an attraction called Medieval Times.

We loaded our suitcases into the car and set off for the twelve-hour drive. We played the "alphabet game," the "I thank Jesus for" game, and, in times of desperation, the "quiet game."

My husband John, the boy's bonus dad, was excited to announce we would be entering Las Vegas ahead of schedule. Around that same time, he made a joke about how horrible it would be if our car broke down in Death Valley; mind you, it was August, and the temperature had climbed to 115 degrees that day.

As we approached Death Valley, the car started surging back and forth. I laughed out loud. I thought my husband had taken his joke to another level until I saw steam pouring out of the engine. When we could no longer see out of the windshield for the steam, we looked at each other wide-eyed and immediately pulled the car over. With the boy's help, I gathered all the water bottles we had brought and gave them to my husband. We watched him pour them one by one into the engine as he tried to cool it down.

The boys and I looked around to see if there was any help in sight. We saw a gas station at the very top of a high hill to our right. We were relieved and excited! Once the engine had cooled, we piled back into the car, and my husband turned it on just long enough to get us to the top of the hill. Our excitement soon turned to disappointment. The gas station was completely boarded up, and there was not a soul in sight! My husband and I looked at each other again wide-eyed.

I was determined to make what could have been a disaster into a good learning experience for my boys. How could I do this? I didn't complain about how hot it was, and I didn't get mad at my husband. It wasn't his fault we were stranded in Death Valley. I gathered my boys close to me and told them that we needed to pray. After we all took a turn praying to Jesus, I assured them that everything would be okay.

It wasn't too long before we could glide our car back down the hill and catch the attention of a highway patrol officer. The officer called a tow truck for us, and then the real waiting began. It was back to the "I thank Jesus for" game.

We were all excited when we finally saw the lights of the tow truck coming in the distance. We cheered until it pulled up alongside us. We waited outside of the car as the tow truck driver loaded our car onto his truck, and then we all piled into the cab. My youngest son looked at me in amazement as he read the tow truck driver's name badge attached to his shirt. "Mom!" he exclaimed, "We prayed, and Jesus came." The tow truck driver's name was Jesus, pronounced "hay-SOOS" in Spanish.

We didn't make it to Las Vegas earlier than expected, but we did get to see the sign "Welcome to Las Vegas" from the view of a tow truck, and the boys thought that was impressive!

Have you ever had something go wrong, but you could make it better just by changing your attitude towards it? Do you have a bad attitude about something now? Thank the Lord every morning this week for all you have, and ask Him to reveal to you any areas you need His help to change. Ask the Lord to help you change those areas, and He will.

19
The Sticky Note

The integrity of the upright guides them, but the unfaithful are destroyed by their duplicity. Proverbs 11:3

Before my mom died, I asked her if I could have her pink Bible, and she said yes. I had seen her reading and writing in that Bible for as long as I could remember. I really couldn't imagine a better place to learn more about the Lord than in her Bible, surrounded by all her study notes.

When my mom went to be with our Lord and Savior, my husband picked up my mom's Bible from the tray that had been beside her for the last eight days and took it home with him. Later I found out that my sister's husband was also going to try to grab the Bible for my sister. She didn't know I had asked our mom for it, and I really couldn't blame her, but I was glad my husband had grabbed it first.

As we heavy-heartedly cleaned out my mom's home, we started noticing sticky notes on the bottom of everything. As we lifted some items, the sticky notes would fall off and float across the room as they had been there for a very long time, and their stickiness had worn off. Sometimes it was hard to figure out where they had come from or read the name on them, but we did our best. There wasn't much for us to go through as my mom lived a simple life, but she had some items she wanted to be sure went to certain family members, so we respected that.

Months went by, and I found myself in church on a Sunday morning holding my mom's pink Bible. I missed her. A substitute pastor was teaching that Sunday, and I must admit my mind had begun to wander. My mom's Bible cover had a pocket in it, and for the first time since she had died, I started going through it. "Interesting…" I thought as I pulled out an old piece of juicy fruit gum. A clear memory of my mother popping more than one piece of juicy fruit gum into her mouth at the same time and blowing bubbles came to my mind and made me smile. It also made me wonder what else was in that pocket. I dug deeper. I found several Bible verses written on small pieces of paper, and I could tell by the writing they were written after her stroke. I found a large paper clip, an old photocopy of a picture of me, and then, "Oh no!" I held my gasp to not interrupt those attentively listening to the teaching. It was a sticky note, and it didn't have my name on it! It read, "Nathaniel!" I stuck it back into the pocket of my mom's pink Bible as fast as I could, as if I'd never seen it and I didn't see it again for another two months.

I justified it. I rationalized it. I knew it must have been some sort of mistake. The sticky note was probably written before I asked for the Bible, so therefore it'd been canceled out.

Two months later, after having forgotten about the sticky note with Nathaniel's name on it pushed deep into my mom's Bible cover pocket, I was in church again. The sermon had just ended, and we stood for the closing prayer. I thought about who I should leave my mom's Bible to when I go to be with my Lord and Savior. I was debating between my youngest son and my oldest. "Who would treasure it the most?" I asked myself.

I opened my eyes at the end of the prayer, and I could not believe what I saw. The sticky note had floated down to the carpet, and it was lying face-up.

"Nathaniel!" it read. I knew then that God had given me this Bible because I would be faithful to give it away to the person my mom wanted to have it, her grandson Nathaniel.

Meditate on the following questions for a few minutes each morning this week and ask God to bring the correct answers to your mind.

What have others trusted you with? What do others depend on you for?

How do the choices you make affect others? How can you make Godly choices that align with God's will, even when you might not want to? How can you continue to honor a loved one's memory who has gone on ahead of you? Does it make a difference if they were a Christian? How can you honor them if you have had differences? Has God been repeatedly speaking with you about someone or something?

Write down anything He tells you and pray according to what He puts on your heart. He's always ready to listen.

PART 2

Man Seeks God

The Lord looks down from heaven on all mankind, to see if there are any who understand, any who seek God.
Psalm 14:2

20
Christian Service

Not giving up meeting together, as some are in the habit of doing, but encouraging one another – and all the more as you see the day approaching. Hebrews 10:25

One Sunday, my pastor let the congregation know the church needed some additional greeters. He talked about what type of person they were looking for, and I could have sworn he looked over at me. Even if it was only my imagination, I knew it was a good fit. I have heard greeters say, "Oh, I didn't do much, I just greeted," but I know the importance of a greeting and how what may seem like the least of volunteer jobs can sometimes be the greatest. My service has been rewarding.

If it hadn't been for stepping out when I heard God's call to service, I never would have met some fantastic people who have deeply touched and impacted my life.

Bless and be blessed.

One of those exceptional people is Rob/Bob. I called him Rob/Bob because I noticed as many people calling him Rob as there were calling him Bob. When I tried to clarify his name, he told me they were correct. As his comments often did, this one made me laugh. He said his closest friends call him Bob, so that is the name I chose to call him.

Bob

Feeling at home on the couch
He sat in his chair
Two halves of a sandwich
Were ours to share.

I had put his on a red plate
That said, "You are special today."
He chose the Fritos
Next to his sandwich, they lay.

I had met my new friend
A few months before
As he made his way through the parking lot
Then through my door.

I'd been a greeter at church
For quite awhile
He said I made coming to church more fun
That made me smile.

I was pleasantly surprised
When he said it'd be okay
To come by his place
To visit someday.

"When was it?" I asked
As I took my first bite
"When you came to trust in Jesus?"
"When you were drawn to the light?"

He told me about his childhood
How Jesus he'd received
When he first became a dad
Teaching his children to believe.

I admired the little glass bird in the cabinet
Lighthouse plates on his wall
Enjoying conversation about family trips
As they were recalled.

He told me of a time
He was kayaking and fell out
When he got to the bottom
He wondered what all the fuss was about.

He asked the emergency personnel
"What's going on?"
"An 80-year-old man floated downstream
And now he's gone."

It was then with a crinkled nose
Head slightly tilted back
The laughter billowed out of him
And I realized it was that!

That laughter, that crinkle,
Had endeared me to him
When he'd walked through my door
Time and time again.

All the while nestled behind me
As I sat on his couch
Was a calico he called "Cat"
Sleeping soundly over tales of fishing for trout.

After we'd finished eating
With silver spoons once belonging to his dad
We stirred instant Folgers
It wasn't half bad.

The highlight of my day
Was when he asked if I'd like
To ride through the neighborhood
On his new three-wheeled bike.

I didn't refuse
I thought it'd be fun
To tuck in my long dress
To ride in the sun.

I laughed as I rode
I must be a sight
With my long dress tucked in
I rode with delight.

Back in the house
My eyes welled up with tears
As he spoke of his Tommy
Who he'd loved for 58 years.

"She didn't leave me much."
He pointed to his left
"Except for her walker," he chuckled
But our time together was my best.

I gave him two cookies
When it was time to go
"I can't eat these," he said
But there's someone who can that I know."

When I left, it felt good
To know how much he was loved
By his two sons, sweet daughter Lorelei,
And our Savior above.

In loving memory of Robert Alvin Sweet

September 14, 1934 – May 7, 2022

Has God been calling you to a place of service? Think about where and how you can serve. Ask for the Lord's direction in this area of your life this week. Ask Him to give you the confidence and courage to step out in faith as He leads you.

If you are already serving and have grown weary in your service, ask God to renew your zest for what He has called you to do. Ask for His blessing and His direction as you serve in this area. Think about why you started serving in this area in the first place and ask God to renew your passion.

Mary

Now you are the body of Christ, and each one of you is a part of it. 1 Corinthians 12:17

Looking like a glamourous Hollywood actress
In head-to-toe class
She came through my door
With an abundance of sass.

As I got to know her each Sunday
In that minute or two
There was something about Mary
For whom my heart grew.

I hugged her one morning
The words spilling out
"I love you, Mary."
She shared her doubts.

I sat with her in church
We planned to have tea
A lift to my heart
When she said, "I love you" to me.

I went to her house
The street name so suitable
A "Lighthouse Lane" to others
Mary's wisdom irrefutable.

"I've been praying for a friend," she shared
So had I!
We laughed at our unlikely pairing
Then we started to cry.

Unlikely, yet perfect
This friendship He'd chosen
A great reminder to us
His love is deeper than the ocean.

Written a few years later…

The last time I saw Mary
Her sons made us some tea
We all laughed, we all cried
Creating a beautiful memory.

Written after she passed away from cancer…

Sitting outside
Up before dawn
I think of you
With my sweater on.

Using the last teabag
From our favorite tea
The name of the flavor
So fittingly.

Called sweet and spicy
You bought me a box
I remember drinking it
In our yellow socks.

My mama Mary
You quickly became
Without you at my door
Church won't be the same.

I am sure going to miss you this side of heaven.

In loving memory of my Mama Mary Shugart

October 19, 1932 - January 19, 2022

Read I Corinthians 12:12-27. Do you have a church home where you can meet people like Bob and Mary? If not, take a moment to ask the Lord to lead you to a good church where you can grow in His Word and have fellowship. Consider serving in your current church or, if you have stopped attending church altogether, returning to your home church or visiting a new church this week.

Have you wanted to attend church regularly but have been putting it off? If so, why? Is it fear, other commitments, or a lack of discipline that keeps you from going? Ask the Lord to help you with whatever is standing in your way and make time for the things that have an eternal impact.

It would be an injustice if I didn't mention the impact church and anointed Bible study teachers have had on my journey as a Christian. Time spent with other believers has also been crucial in my walk with the Lord. We can't do it on our own. We aren't supposed to.

21
Romans Chapter 8

We know that the whole creation has been groaning as in the pains of childbirth right up to the present time. Romans 8:22

One hot day in July, I came home from church and tossed my open Bible gently on the couch next to my dog of almost 12 years, Oliver. The sofa in the front room had become one of his favorite spots to lie, and I could find him there most days now when I came home from work or play. That day, when I laid the Bible down next to him, he yawned, took a big stretch, laid his head down on the open Bible, and looked directly up at me. I had a few Bibles over the years, but this one was extraordinary, a treasure left to me by my mother.

As Oliver took that big stretch and laid his head down on my mom's Bible, I grabbed my iPhone and took a quick picture. I reviewed the photo, decided it was nothing remarkable, and went about my day.

Thanksgiving was a warm and sunny day that year, so I brought Oliver outside to sit on the front porch. My husband and my very handy bonus son were putting up the Christmas lights before we headed over to my niece's home for Thanksgiving dinner. I enjoyed watching Oliver spread out on his orthopedic mattress and soak up the sun. It was a perfect day.

When we returned home, we noticed Oliver's breathing had become labored. By the following day, we knew something was very wrong. We rushed him to the veterinarian, the same one who had seen him since he was eight weeks old. Her words were painful yet straightforward, "It's time."

We called my oldest son first, who came right over, and then we placed a call to England, where my youngest son was stationed in the U.S. Air Force. While I filled him in on Oliver, I was grateful for the times he had been home over the last four years and the many swims Oliver and him had taken during those visits. He insisted on staying on the phone until we had all said our goodbyes.

With almost twelve years of membership, Oliver was one of the family. He had a very special place in the boys' hearts, as he was the dog they had saved their garage sale money to buy. He was the only dog they had had for their entire lives. After saying goodbye, hanging up our phones, and knowing my oldest son was safely home, I sat on my mom's old wicker loveseat that had found a new home on my front porch. I was numb.

As I often did, I began writing a poem from my front porch.

The Garage Sale Dog

All little boys
Should have a dog
My husband wanted no part
In this dialogue.

Why wasn't I happy
To just have a cat?
End of discussion
That would be that!

He finally agreed
But "she" had to be small
A miniature
Or nothing at all.

I told my boys
To gather their stuff
What we could sell
Must be enough.

To send for this dog
A boy's best friend
Their excitement
Reached to no end.

Our garage sale
Was a huge endeavor
I was so proud
As my boys worked harder than ever.

They were delighted
As they counted their money
Just enough for their garage sale dog
Not an extra penny.

When we picked the dog up
From the airport that day
My husband was speechless
What could he say?

This little dog
Wasn't a she
Although he was adorable
It was kind of funny (to me).

When the dog stumbled and fell
Into our spa that first day
We noticed his huge feet
Had gotten in his way.

The dog grew and grew
To over sixty pounds
He wasn't small but the sweetest garage sale dog
We could ever have found.

We all fell in love with him
In every way
Even my husband
Eventually thought he was okay.

He pulled the boys on their skateboards
Loved playing in the pool
Happily greeted them
Every day after school.

Years went by too quickly
My little boys grew to men
The garage sale dog
Remained their best friend.

When they moved out
With a tear in their eyes
A man's best friend now
They said goodbye.

He taught us that friends
Come in many sizes
And sometimes the best things in life
Are the surprises.

Written in remembrance of Oliver
Who was such a big part
Of our family's lives
Forever in our hearts.

Oliver
June 2, 2006 – November 23, 2018

The Lord is close to the brokenhearted and saves those who are crushed in spirit.
Psalm 34:18

Over the past twelve years, Oliver had a lot of fans on Facebook, and I knew they would be sad to hear of his passing. Knowing this made me determined to find the perfect picture to post alongside the poem. I had so many beautiful photos of Oliver on my phone to choose from. Still, when I got to the pictures I had taken back in July, I found the one of Oliver from that warm Sunday after church. This time the image seemed perfect. So on to Facebook, it went.

I had canceled all the plans I had for the long Thanksgiving weekend, and I went between the couch and the front porch for most of it. I just sat there. I was sad. I thought about when my mom had died and how I had asked God for a sign that she was in heaven. The sign I received came miraculously. It was a poem called "I am Now in Heaven." It had fallen out of one of her books and floated down onto the floor in front of me face up. (See "The Sign" in my book, *Let the Son Shine In.*) I asked God for another sign now. Was Oliver in heaven?

Even though I had just gone through a Bible study on heaven a few months earlier, questions remained. As I moved from the couch to the front porch, I had my phone handy, so I started googling whether dogs go to heaven or not. I found a Christian blog that referred to Romans Chapter 8. The blogger used scripture from that chapter to substantiate his belief that dogs do go to heaven. If you have ever loved and lost a dog, you know how comforting this was to me.

As I read the scriptures and prayed, I suddenly remembered the picture of Oliver I had posted a couple of days earlier on Facebook. My mind raced as I scrambled to find it. Where had my Bible been opened to? When I saw the picture, I magnified it to get a closer look. I could not believe my eyes!

Oliver's head was resting on Romans Chapter 8!

Can you recall a time in your life when you were brokenhearted? Maybe that time is now. What did God do to remind you of His closeness? What can you do to experience the intimacy of God this week?

How can you comfort someone else with the comfort God has given you this week? How can you show them God's love?

22
Walking in God's Favor

God cares about the small things, and everything is small compared to God.

Indeed, the very hairs of your head are all numbered. Don't be afraid; you are worth more than many sparrows. Luke 12:7

I woke up extra early, grabbed my Bible and my daily devotion book, and crawled back into bed like any other day. The time I set aside faithfully every morning to spend with the Lord is precious to me. A few moments later, and much to my delight, my husband brought up a fresh cup of coffee and placed it on my nightstand. On this particular day, I was three books into the Old Testament, and I was eager to find out what happened next. I read a few chapters out of Leviticus, a beautiful devotional out of Streams in the Desert by L.B. Cowman, which my pastor's wife had recently recommended, and I prayed.

As soon as I took my last sip of deliciousness, I looked at the clock and headed for the shower. It wasn't until I was in the shower that I noticed my left diamond earring was missing. My heart sank. The earrings resulted from a memorable surprise trip to the jewelry store with my husband. The sentimental value was irreplaceable.

I quickly got out of the shower, and my quest to find the diamond earring began. I looked everywhere! I looked under the mattress, on top of the mattress, and everywhere in between. I ran my fingers through each blanket, bed sheet, bedspread, and the carpet below. My heart began to lift a little when I found the back to the earring on my bottom sheet, but it quickly sank again as I scoured the rest of the sheet and found nothing.

I prayed a prayer I have prayed on numerous occasions, asking the Lord to have favor on me and that the lost be found because He knows where everything is. Over the years, God has answered that prayer for me many times. I can't count how many misplaced baseball mitts I have found at the last minute, right in time for the big game, and in some pretty strange places.

When my husband returned from taking our new rescue dog outside, he came upstairs to help me. We re-searched every area on our hands and knees together, going over every inch of the carpet. I was so confident God would help me right then and there I didn't put on any other earrings until, with one last glance in the bathroom and only five minutes to spare, I had no other choice. I put on a pretty pair of blue topaz earrings a dear friend had given me. "My diamond earring just couldn't have gone down the drain and be lost forever," I thought as I walked out my front door.

Feeling a little deflated by this time, I got in my car and headed towards work. I turned on my usual 8:00 a.m. to 8:30 a.m. radio program, In Touch Ministries with Charles Stanley. I listened to it every weekday unless I had to get into the office earlier than usual.

With my earring still in the forefront of my mind, I listened half-heartedly as Charles Stanley talked about the sanctity of prayer and what it means to pray in Jesus' name. I told the Lord with a loud sigh, "Come on! What good is one earring? I can't do anything with one earring, and what good could it possibly do to lose it?" When the broadcast ended, I quieted myself, and I prayed again how Charles Stanley had just described so perfectly, "In Jesus' name." As soon as I parked my car in the parking garage at work, I texted my husband. It read, "Please check again. Please!!!!"

I retold my earring story several times to anyone who would listen. Then I got busy with my regular duties and conference calls. The day was a typical day, except my earrings were blue. As it got close to 3:30 p.m., I received a picture in a text message from my husband. I couldn't figure out what it was at first. I turned the image in several directions and tried to zoom in, but it was still blurry. Another picture came over about this time, and I could see a hole and a pipe.

My husband explained that he had removed the filter in the shower, so the pipe was exposed. And there it was! Perfectly balanced on a tiny ¼ inch lip next to the pipe sat my beautiful but rather slimy diamond earring. Tears filled my eyes as I showed my co-workers that my earring had indeed been found!

As I walked back into my office, I thanked the Lord for caring about the "little" things that concern us. It was then that I heard a familiar voice with a gentle reminder, "I will never leave you or forsake you." I thanked Him harder.

Whatever small or large thing troubles your heart this week, remember that God cares. He is willing to do everything He has done for me for you. I encourage you to immediately give any trouble that arises this week to God. Experience the peace that surpasses all understanding. It is a gift from God to those who believe in Him.

If you find yourself taking your worries back, give them over to the Lord as many times as you need to. Thank Him for what He is doing behind the scenes that you may not be aware of in your current situation. He's there for you. He's working on your behalf, and He will never leave you.

23
The Sting of Rejection

Even if my father and mother abandon me, the Lord will hold me close. Psalm 27:10

If the world hates you, keep in mind that it hated me first. John 15:18

When his people pray for help, he listens and rescues them from their troubles. The Lord is there to rescue all who are discouraged and have given up hope. The Lord's people may suffer a lot, but he will always bring them safely through. Not one of their bones will be broken. Psalm 34: 17-20

Feeling the sting of rejection for the umpteenth time, I found myself on my knees on my bedroom floor before the Lord. This most recent occurrence had happened four months earlier, but the time that followed had seemed painstakingly long. I had pleaded with the Lord, "I don't understand this. I've been kind. I've done everything right, and I don't want to feel this way anymore! I beg of you to help me let this go. It breaks my heart every day, and I can do nothing about it." I felt resigned to carry this burden with me for the rest of my life. I thought about the thorn in Paul's flesh in 2 Corinthians 12:6-7 and wondered if this would be mine.

As I started my car that morning, the radio was tuned to one of my favorite stations, Bott Radio Network. The tail end of Charles Stanley's program was on. I had been to a Bible study on spiritual gifts a few months earlier, and this was what today's program was about. I had been waiting for the last two weeks for Charles Stanley to discuss my spiritual gift. He had discussed each spiritual gift separately and had not gotten to mine yet. Although I had missed the program's first half, I heard exactly what I needed to hear that morning as I pulled out of my driveway. "The people with this gift close their spirits off to insensitive people." he said, "They simply can't handle it. They get hurt more than any other spiritual gift." It was my gift, the gift of mercy, that he was talking about and one of the quickest answers I have ever received from the Lord. It all made sense now why I was hurting over this situation. I still didn't know what else to do in this trial, but I suddenly understood myself in a way I never had before. I even appreciate my younger self better.

I later learned that all you have to do in a trial is bow down, worship, and be still.

God always answers when we ask Him for something. His answer may be yes, but sometimes He tells us to wait. Other times He may gently say, "I have something better in store for you." Ask God, "Do you have something better for me?" Thank Him this week for the prayer requests He didn't say yes to, trusting that He is sovereign, all-knowing, and working all things out for your good and His perfect purpose.

Not long after this teaching on Bott Radio Network, I learned that God also answers us in another way. If God doesn't say yes, or wait, or I have something better for you, He may take your desire for what you are praying for away. That is what He did for me in this instance. Not only did He take my desire for what I wanted away, but I also have never felt hurt or bitter over it.

24
Because He Cares We Can Face Tomorrow

And we know that in all things God works for the good of those who love him, who have been called according to his purpose.
Romans 8:28

Soon after adopting a curly, creme-colored miniature Goldendoodle from a local no-kill shelter named Charlie, my niece started declaring, as he enthusiastically enjoyed a new toy or a chew stick, that "This is his best life!"

Hearing the tapping of his tail against the couch when he'd see me coming down the stairs in the morning, the way he would push his head deep into the crook of my arm to keep his little black nose warm while I was reading my Bible in the early hours, and the way he would perk up every Friday when he heard the words "Yuppy Puppy," knowing he would soon be on his way to the groomers, were all reasons I had grown to love him deeply.

As the months passed and behaviors he had developed while in the shelter began to surface, we had to make the excruciating decision that he wasn't a good fit for our family. I was heartbroken as we tried our hardest to find him a one-person home, and even the no-kill shelter wouldn't take him back. They said we would probably have to put him to sleep. The thought of that was unbearable for me.

I was out of town on business the following week, and it was there, in the privacy of my hotel room, that I got on my knees and poured my aching heart out to the Lord, "Please find him a home." I begged. "It's hard enough to let him go, but somehow Lord let him live out his best life." I cried.

It was just two days later when my husband got the call. One of the groomers from Yuppy Puppy would be taking him, and we were welcome to visit him there any time! Bittersweet tears rolled down my cheeks as I heard the news. "How many dogs get adopted by a groomer!?" I asked myself as I looked up and thanked the Arranger. "Instead of going to the groomer one day a week, he can go five days a week for free!"

Don't ever think God doesn't care about everything in your life.

Please pray with me. "Thank you for making a way when there seems to be no way. When our means are inadequate, Lord, thank you for caring and providing for us."

Make a list of all the ways God is adequate this week. How has He shown He cares for you? How has He provided for you? How has He watched over you? Has He ever protected you when you didn't realize you needed His protection until later?

Fourteen days after finding a new owner for Charlie, I was facing a more significant challenge, one that would test my faith.

25
He Speaks to Us

In the past God spoke to our ancestors through the prophets at many times and in various ways, but in the last days he has spoken to us by his Son, whom he appointed heir of all things, and through whom also he made the universe. Hebrews 1:1-2

It was the beginning of 2020, and I was preparing to go on a big trip with my church. The tour was called "The Footsteps of Paul," and we would be touring Greece, Turkey, and Italy. It was exciting to think I would be standing where the apostle Paul stood in just a matter of weeks! As I laid out my travel clothes, I heard a very distinctive voice; it wasn't audible, but it was clear: "Why are you wasting your time?" He asked, "You aren't going on this trip." If I wasn't going on this trip, surely no one was, I thought.

God still speaks to us today. He speaks to us through His Word, prayer, and trusted advisors. He gives us a sense of peace when we take time to sit quietly before Him, listen, and obey His will. He opens and closes doors to keep us from walking out of His will, and speaks to us through His still, small voice inside our hearts.

Reflect on a time you knew God was speaking to you and thank Him for it. If you need to hear from God on any topic today, ask Him now and listen expectantly for the still, small voice this week. Feed your spirit on His Word as you wait and worship, and remember to write down what He says to you.

26
He Puts People in Our Paths

For I know the plans I have for you," declares the Lord, "plans to prosper you and not to harm you, plans to give you hope and a future. Jeremiah 29:11

I had only been asked to be a part of the women's ministry leadership team a short time before, and I didn't know many of the ladies that well yet. But as we sat in a circle sharing a verse or word the Lord had given us for 2020, I was immediately drawn to one of the ladies in the group. It wasn't only what she shared; but how she shared it. In a very gracious, becoming way and choosing her words carefully, she told us she was going through the most arduous trial of her life. My heart went out to her. I thought of my most challenging trial, when my husband sat on the couch next to me and told me he didn't love me anymore. It was 1999, and he was leaving our two little boys and me for the third time.

As this lady came to my mind over the next few weeks, and she often did, I prayed for her. I didn't know the specifics of her trial, but I knew the Lord did, and He cared about every little detail of it. I thought about texting her a couple of times, but then, surprisingly, she texted me! She told me she was thinking about something I had said to the group the last time we met. My words, "Don't let your love dim," encouraged her to keep shining her light even amid her own dark trial.

I had no idea what a difference being a part of this Christian women's group would make in my life in just 35 days.

February 3, 2020, was like any other day, except I was rushing back from lunch to go to a doctor's appointment. I received a reminder card a couple of weeks earlier and hadn't wasted any time making the appointment. I had gotten a mammogram every year, and although I found them uncomfortable and sometimes even a little painful, this time, the technician got me in and out so quickly that I barely felt it. I was back to work within the hour.

The first call of many came the following day. The doctor's office wanted to know if I could come back in at 3:15 p.m. I was surprised by the short notice, but I was not the least bit concerned. I knew the technician had rushed me through the previous day, and I assumed it was because she didn't get a good image. I didn't get home until 6:30 that evening. By then, I'd had a second mammogram, an ultrasound, and three painful biopsies. Had I heard them correctly? If the three biopsies were cancerous, they wouldn't have to biopsy the other two deeper areas. Would they assume those were cancer, too? And why did the radiologist ask me to wait after the others told me I could leave and then call me into her office to show me the images she was looking at? Was she supposed to do that? My head was spinning, but I still wasn't worried. Breast cancer didn't run in my family.

Reflect on a time God put someone in your path, made your way straight (Provers 3:5-6), or used another person to sharpen you (Proverbs 27:17) and write it down. If you have more than one past reflection, write them down. Don't forget to thank God for each one as you go about your week.

27
He Prepares Us

For he says to Moses, "I will have mercy on whom I have mercy, and I will have compassion on whom I have compassion." It does not, therefore, depend on human desire or effort, but on God's mercy. For Scripture says to Pharaoh: "I raised you up for this very purpose, that I might display my power in you and that my name might be proclaimed in all the earth." Therefore God has mercy on whom he wants to have mercy, and he hardens whom he wants to harden. Romans 9:15-18

Beloved, think it not strange concerning the fiery trial which is to try you, as though some strange thing happened unto you: But rejoice, inasmuch as ye are partakers of Christ's sufferings; that, when his glory shall be revealed, ye may be glad also with exceeding joy. 1 Peter 4:12-13

And we know that in all things God works for the good of those who love him, who have been called according to his purpose. Romans 8:28

On February 6, 2020, I woke up early, as usual, and headed downstairs for my quiet time. Along with my Bible, I was reading a devotional book a friend had lent me called, "*My Utmost for His Highest"* by Oswald Chambers. As I read, "Are you ready to be poured out as an offering?" God spoke to me as He had so many times before. But this time, I didn't like what He was saying, "It is an act of your will, not your emotions. Tell God without any complaints, despite what God may send your way. You must be willing to be placed on the altar and go through the fire; willing to experience what the altar represents – burning, purification, and separation for only one purpose – the elimination of every desire and affection not grounded in or directed toward God. But you don't eliminate it, God does. You 'bind the sacrifice… to the horns of the altar' and see to it that you don't wallow in self-pity once the fire begins. After you have gone through the fire, there will be nothing that will be able to trouble or depress you. When another crisis arises, you will realize that things cannot touch you as they used to do. Tell God you are ready to be poured out as an offering, and God will prove Himself to be all you ever dreamed He would be."

I said "No" to the pointed question in the devotional and promptly got in the shower. I wasn't ready, but I took the devotional book to work with me that morning and reread it at my desk. I already knew when my phone rang with both the radiologist and the breast health nurse on the line later that afternoon.

"You have cancer." one of them said.

I didn't cry out but instead decided to tell my staff immediately. I still wonder "who" said what came out of my mouth next, "God has been preparing me for this for a long time." But He had.

By Friday that same week, my husband and I sat before a team of seven doctors. They told me I had stage 2a invasive ductal carcinoma, that it was HER2+ and hormone negative, and it had affected at least one of my lymph nodes. My treatment would include chemotherapy, a mastectomy, and radiation. It was all happening so fast.

The lyrics to the song "Truth I'm Standing On" by Leanna Crawford came to mind. Please take a few minutes to listen to this song now.

I don't remember much else about that appointment, but Sunday evening, I went up for prayer after church. I was anointed with oil, and there stood the same lady I had been drawn to from the women's ministry group. She gave me the longest and warmest hug.

I met with the breast health nurse the following week. As soon as my husband and I walked into her office, I noticed the book *"Jesus Calling"* on the shelf above her desk. The book held special meaning to me because a friend had given me a copy of it a year earlier after surviving throat cancer. I was surprised and comforted when at the end of the meeting, the nurse took the book down from the shelf and read that day's devotion to me:

I AM TAKING CARE OF YOU. Feel the warmth and security of being enveloped in My loving Presence. Every detail of your life is under My control. Moreover, *everything fits into a pattern for good to those who love Me and are called according to My design and purpose.* Because the world is in an abnormal, fallen condition, people tend to think that chance governs the universe. Events may seem to occur randomly, with little or no meaning. People who view the world this way have overlooked one basic fact: the limitations of human understanding. What you know of the world you inhabit is only the tip of the iceberg. Submerged beneath the surface of the visible world are mysteries too vast for you to comprehend. If you could only see how close I am to you and how constantly I work on your behalf, you would never again doubt that I am wonderfully caring for you. This is why you must live *by faith, not by sight,* trusting in My mysterious, majestic Presence.

The devotion was from Romans 8:28. I glanced at my left wrist, where I have a simple tattoo that reads Romans 8.

I encourage you to sit before the Lord this week, read the eighth chapter of Romans, and ask God to speak to you through His Word. List how He speaks to you and how you can apply it to your daily life. God's Word never returns void.

28
He Uses the Least of These

When you pass through the waters, I will be with you; and when you pass through the rivers, they will not sweep over you. When you walk through the fire, you will not be burned; the flames will not set you ablaze. Isaiah 43:2

Not knowing how long I might be away from work, I went downstairs with a trusted co- worker to talk and get something to eat during our lunch break. The restaurant we wanted to go to was packed, so my co-worker suggested we cross the street and go to a less crowded restaurant, but knowing how much she loved what we had come to call the "Leslie Bowl" from the restaurant we were already at, I insisted we stay. We could see there was one table left on the back patio, but it had already been taken by the time the waitress asked the server if we could sit there. Desperate to return to work within an hour, my friend pointed out four empty chairs and two tables in the front of the restaurant on a barely enclosed sidewalk. With a sigh, we sat down. It was better than nothing.

My co-worker and I had been friends since 1989, and we often shared glimpses of God's great love for us that we call "Jesus kisses." But this time, our conversation centered around cancer. We noticed a homeless man approaching as we waited for our food to be brought to our table. He didn't stop until he was right next to me! I was not expecting the words that came out of his mouth when he leaned in and said, "Jesus is with you." I sat there stunned. Had he just said what I thought he said? My friend confirmed it. It gave us both chills. God never disappoints us, and this was a very unexpected "Jesus kiss."

How has Jesus shown you that He cares about every little detail of your life? How has He shown you that He is there and involved in your day-to-day?

Ask the Lord to make you aware of "Jesus kisses" this week and write them down as He does. Before you go on to next week's devotion, thank God for every "kiss" He sends.

29
God Makes a Beautiful Tapestry Out of Our Circumstances

Oft' times He
weaveth sorrow;
And I in foolish pride
Forget He sees the upper
And I the underside. – Grant Colfax Tullar

Later that week, immense joy came over me as I felt a gentle nudge telling me to give my Footsteps of Paul trip away. I contacted the travel agency, and the gentleman on the phone told me I could gift my trip. He also went a step further when he prayed for me to find the perfect person to take my place. Once I got the go-ahead from the travel agency, I asked my pastor's wife if she knew anyone who would like to go on the trip in my place. "Of course!" I said out loud when she said the lady's name. It was the same lady from the women's ministry group that I had been drawn to, the one I had been praying for, who had given me a hug that Sunday evening when I had gone forward at church. She was the lady that was supposed to go on this trip! I didn't want her to know I was giving her the trip, but the pastor's wife encouraged me to tell her because she said she would need to understand how this had all come about. I talked to my husband, who was saddened that I couldn't go on the trip but agreed that if I couldn't go and wanted to give the trip away, someone else should benefit from it. I texted the lady, not mentioning the trip, but to set up a day and time we could talk on the phone. Twenty minutes before that scheduled call, my sister called me.

To my surprise, my sister asked me who one of the leaders in the women's ministry group was, and her description was that of the same leader I was supposed to call in twenty minutes! "I had the weirdest thing happen last night," she said, "I couldn't fall asleep because I kept thinking about that leader. She was very hesitant about something, but I kept seeing her in Israel. She was super happy, and so were you." This was complete confirmation, as my sister knew nothing about me giving my trip away yet. I excitedly filled her in on the details, "It wasn't Israel." I told her, but I was sure my sister had just gotten that confused with Italy, Greece, or Turkey. (It did end up being Israel, but I will get to that later.) I couldn't wait to call this lady and share this amazing story with her! Sure enough, in her gracious, becoming way with carefully chosen words that I had come to admire, she said she could not accept the gift. As we continued to talk, she shared with me that she had just renewed her passport. I asked her to pray about accepting the trip, and I told her that I would continue praying about it, too. We agreed she would call me back after careful consideration. When she declined the gift a second time, I asked her one question, "Why did you renew your passport?" She said she wasn't sure; maybe she was going to visit her daughter overseas. I excitedly told her that I knew why she had renewed her passport! "You are going to walk in the footsteps of Paul!"

I said, and she accepted.

Having been given a couple of choices; chemotherapy or surgery first and which chemotherapy regimen to choose, I sought a second opinion from UCSF. Once I confirmed that the opinion of my surgeon and UCSF were the same, I put myself on a cancellation list to receive a port for the infusions. I started my chemotherapy on March 2, 2020. The treatments would be given every three weeks for four and a half months. I'd be scheduled for a mastectomy four weeks after the chemotherapy ended and radiation every day for twenty-three days eight weeks after the surgery. The road looked daunting.

The song Faithful God, by the group I Am They came to mind.

I am surrounded
On every side
Can't see the light of day
But I am persuaded
Beyond all hope, You won't let go of me
I stake my claim on every word You say
You will not be late

I will sing through fire and thunder
'Cause You are on my side, I trust You with my life
I know my story, it isn't over
Even against all odds
You are a faithful God
You're faithful God

The darkest of weather
Though I can’t see, I still believe You’re good
So I’m moving forward
Through crashin’ waves
I know I’m safe with You
You hold my life
You hear my cry
With every breath inside

I will sing through fire and thunder
‘Cause You are on my side, I trust You with my life
I know my story, it isn’t over
Even against all odds
Oh, You are a faithful God (yeah)
That’s who You are

Oh, You are a faithful God
Oh, You’re a faithful God

What does it mean to you to be surrounded on every side?

Read the poem "The Weaver" by Grant Colfax Tullar.

Read Psalm 31 this week. Did David ever feel surrounded? If so, what was his reaction to God during these times?

Do you trust Him with your life?

Sit still before the Lord for a few minutes every day this week and say, "Lord, please speak to me." Then listen quietly for His voice.

30
He Takes Care of Everything!

But he said to me, "My grace is sufficient for you, for my power is made perfect in weakness. Therefore I will boast all the more gladly of my weaknesses, so that Christ's power may rest on me." 2 Corinthians 12:9

I'm not going to lie. The road was long and dark and daunting, and my prayer requests were many. I prayed for healing, that I could tolerate the side effects from the treatments, for successful surgeries, and for reconstruction, which was considered elective surgery during COVID-19. I had read somewhere that God covers our heads to show His loving kindness towards us, so I prayed for a little bit of hair to be left too. It didn't take me long to realize that I had never really learned how to sit completely still. Now I had no choice. It was God, cancer, and me.

The isolation required from having a compromised immune system, combined with the COVID-19 restrictions put on the state of California in March 2020, was one of the hardest things I have ever had to go through. When I was feeling better, there was no one to see and nowhere to go, but there were flowers and small gifts left on my front porch from time to time that kept me from feeling completely alone. When the cards started coming, I was so glad they did! Some days it was all I could do to walk to the mailbox, and that walk was something I started looking forward to.

My co-workers, pastor and his wife, family, friends, and ladies from the church checked on me regularly through text messages and phone calls. Some brought my family food, while others brought gift cards for restaurants.

My sisters visited often. One helped me remember when to take my medicine, helped with sponge baths and laundry, and at the end of the day, we would share what we were grateful for. My other sister brought unsweetened green teas and sat next to me at the dining room table as she pressed stick-on nails to the end of each of my fingers. We eventually progressed to toenails.

I had difficulty concentrating after my treatments, so I listened to Bible scriptures on tape and K-Love on the radio. I reflected on other seasons in my life when God had been faithful, and I could see in this season that my every need was being met.

My youngest son encouraged me by crossing off each treatment from an appointment calendar as I completed them. He checked off the first one and then chose a cross, a heart, and a Star of David to check off the others. He sat on the side of my bed and read to me. My husband became very good at giving injections. He gave me thirty in all.

Whenever I felt up to it, I would take long walks and ride my favorite yellow bike like I did before I got sick. I started taking Bible verses written on index cards along with me on my walks. I prayed them, claimed them, and tried to memorize them. Other times I thanked God for each promise one by one.

I looked forward to rides with my husband. Sometimes we'd just run errands, and although I couldn't go in anywhere because of my compromised immune system and COVID-19, it felt so good to get out! When we'd go to Lowe's, he'd park me in front of the flowers.

My great-nieces and nephews drew pictures for me that my niece or sister would drop off. Once they made me a big sign that read, "We love you, Aunt Leslie!" and taped it to the front window facing the kitchen. It had little stick-on crosses surrounding it. It was such a wonderful surprise when I looked out my front window for the first time since they had put it there, and the crosses were such a sweet reminder of God's great love for me.

Then there were the hummingbirds. They reminded my sister and me of our mom. I had never successfully attracted hummingbirds, but now they were everywhere! I was even given a second hummingbird feeder from my nephew. I watched them every day in the front and back yard. I watched as the babies were born and as they flew away.

I thought about Luke 12:7, "And even the very hairs on your head are all numbered," and I cried the first day my hair started falling out in the shower. My oldest son and I FaceTimed for a long time that day, and he said, "Mom, maybe you should take control and shave your head." He even offered to do it. I had never had long, thick beautiful hair, so I couldn't donate it, but I asked the Lord, "What can I do with my hair?" And then the thought of a baby bird snuggling up in one of my curls made me smile, so I put locks of my hair as high as I could reach in the trees in my yard, hoping the birds would use it to make their nests.

When I could, I concentrated on others. Each morning, I asked God to use me to bless someone else. I didn't know how I was going to do this from home, but He helped me find ways. One day I saw a new neighbor pushing her mom in a wheelchair down the street like I used to do with my mom. I ran into my house, grabbed a copy of a book I'd written in 2018 called "Let the Son Shine In" and ran out to give it to her. I saw her weeks later when I was feeling a little down. I was walking around our block when she called from an open upstairs window, "Hey, are you the lady who gave me the book? I've been reading it to my mom daily, and it's beautiful."

During this time, I heard a very touching story about an older man who always wore yellow socks. When he died, his granddaughter started collecting yellow socks in his memory. She said the socks represented God walking with us through the uncomfortable. I had an idea! I bought the fuzziest, brightest yellow socks I could find and made tags with Bible verses on them. It brought me great joy to see the smiles they brought to the other patients, nurses, and their staff as I passed them out at the infusion center.

The morning of my mastectomy, I had to say goodbye to my husband in the waiting room because of the COVID-19 restrictions and walk through the door to a five-and-a-half-hour surgery with a registered nurse. It was scary, but her kindness made a difference. She made sure they knew to give me my glasses as soon as I woke up from surgery because I couldn't see without them, something my husband would have made sure of had he been able to be there. But it was the look of disbelief on her face and what she said as each of my assigned doctors entered the room that I will never forget. She said I had been given all of their very best doctors. But it wasn't until the surgical nurse walked in that her mouth literally fell open. "You haven't just been given all of our very best doctors," she said, "You have been given the very best team we have here! She then hugged the surgical nurse, who was her best friend.

I made it through the chemotherapy with tolerable side effects; I was given the first part of the reconstruction at the time of my mastectomy, which I had been told would probably not happen because of Covid-19 and some hair remained on the top of my head, to remind me of His loving kindness.

On July 17, 2020, I was told I am cancer-free! He is truly the God of the valleys and the God of the mountaintops.

Take a moment to write down your valley and mountaintop experiences this week. What was your most profound valley experience? Is there a moment in your life you describe as a before and after moment, a turning point when you realized you would never be the same, that the event had forever divided your life into before and after this event happened? What was your highest mountaintop experience?

How did God reveal Himself to you in these experiences? If He wasn't a part of your life then, how do you think having a relationship with Him would have made a difference in how you viewed these experiences?

Are you going through a hard time now? Invite Him into the circumstance. Even if you can't feel His presence, He is right there with you. He will use this challenging time for your good and His glory.

Praise Him for what He is doing in your current situation, even if you can't see it. Look to the mountaintops this week and sit still.

31
He Protects Us

He knows, He loves, He cares;
Nothing this truth can dim.
He gives the very best to those
Who leave the choice to Him.
– Grant Colfax Tullar

One day as I was sitting on my front porch, something dawned on me. No one is ever thankful to be given a cancer diagnosis, but I realized God's sovereignty at that moment. My cancer was fast-growing, my job was deemed "essential" during Covid-19, and I felt great! All the professionals said I would never have discovered my cancer on my own. If I hadn't gotten that reminder card in the mail when I did and called right away to schedule my mammogram, there was a good chance I wouldn't have gotten an appointment at all. I had since learned that they were canceling all mammogram appointments because of COVID-19.

Nobody but God could have orchestrated these events. "But God" in a sentence changes everything.

The lyrics of Through All of It by Colton Dixon came to mind. Please take a few minutes to listen to this song and meditate on the beautiful verses. Ask God what He is speaking to you through this song this week.

I have lived to tell you, "He is faithful through all of it."

Suppose you didn't get your mammogram until after Covid, your prayer wasn't answered with the desired outcome, or your cancer spread. If that is the case, it doesn't mean God doesn't love you or that He isn't in control of your circumstances. He does! And He is!

32
God Keeps His Promises

Your kingdom is an everlasting kingdom, and Your dominion endures through all generations. The Lord is trustworthy in all He promises and faithful in all He does. Psalm 145:13

I encourage you to cling to His promises as I did. Write these verses and any others that speak to your heart on index cards and meditate on them. Put them on your desk at work, take them with you on your next walk, thank God for them, claim them as your own, and let the Holy Spirit bring them to your remembrance when you need them the most. The bolded words in the verses below are the words I underlined and emphasized on my scripture cards.

Cast your cares on the Lord, and He **will sustain** you; He will never let the righteous be shaken. Psalm 55:22

God is **our refuge** and **strength**, an ever- present **help** in trouble. Psalm 46:1

The Lord is **good** and His **love endures** forever; His **faithfulness continues** through all generations. Psalm 100:5

For I know the plans I have for you," declares the Lord, "plans to prosper you and not to harm you, plans to give you **hope** and **a future**." Jeremiah 29:11

I can do all this through Him who **gives** me **strength**.
Philippians 4:13

For I am the Lord your God who **takes hold** of your right hand and says to you, "Do not fear; I **will help** you."
Isaiah 41:13

May the God of hope fill you with all joy and peace as you **trust in Him**, so that you may overflow with hope by the **power** of the Holy Spirit.
Romans 15:13

The Lord your God goes with you; He **will never leave** you nor forsake you. Deuteronomy 31:6

The Lord **upholds** all who fall and **lifts up** all who are bowed down.
Psalm 145:14

Be strong and courageous. Do not be afraid; do not be discouraged, for the Lord your God **will be with you** wherever you go.
Joshua 1:9

He **will cover you** with His feathers, and under His wings you will find refuge; His **faithfulness** will be your shield and rampart.
Psalm 91:4

When you lie down, you will not be afraid; when you lie down, your sleep will be sweet.
Proverbs 3:24

The name of the Lord is a **fortified** tower; the righteous run to it and are **safe**.
Proverbs 18:10

The Lord is good, **a refuge** in times of trouble. He **cares** for those who trust in Him,
Nahum 1:7

God's voice thunders in **marvelous** ways; He does **great** things beyond our understanding.
Job 37:5

The Lord is **my strength** and **my shield**; my heart trusts in Him, and He **helps** me.
My heart leaps for joy, and with my song I praise Him.
Psalm 28:7

For the Lord your God **is gracious** and **compassionate**. He **will not turn His face from you** if you return to Him.
2 Chronicles 30:9

You are **my strength**, I sing praise to You; You, God, are **my fortress**, my God **on whom I can rely**.
Psalm 59:17

The righteous cry out, and the Lord **hears** them; He **delivers** them from all their troubles. Psalm 34:17

Your sun will never set again, and your moon will wane no more, the Lord will be your **everlasting light,** and your days of **sorrow will end**. Isaiah 60:20

Even though I walk through the darkest valley, I will fear no evil, for You are **with me**; Your rod and Your staff, they **comfort me**. Psalm 23:4

The Lord is **my rock**, **my fortress** and **my deliverer**; my God is **my rock**, in whom I take **refuge**, **my shield** and the **horn of my salvation**, **my stronghold**. Psalm 18:2

And we know that in all things God **works for the good** of those who love him, who have been called according to His purpose. Romans 8:28

The Lord **will keep** you from all harm – He **will watch over** your life; the Lord will watch over your coming and going both now and forevermore. Psalm 121:7-8

No, in all these things we are more than **conquerors through Him** who loved us. Romans 8:37

Now reread all the words I have bolded in the verses; will sustain, our refuge, strength, good, enduring love, continued faithfulness, hope, a future, gives, strengthens, takes hold, will help, trustworthy, powerful, will never leave, upholds, lifts, is with, will cover, faithful, fortified, safe, cares, marvelous, great, shield, gracious, compassionate, will not turn His face from, fortress, reliable, hears, everlasting light, giver of joy, comforter, rock, deliverer, horn of salvation, stronghold, works for good, will keep, and will watch over. You are a conqueror through Him. You can have all this and more in Him!

Write these words on an index card or a piece of colorful paper and put them on your bathroom mirror or the review mirror in your car. Mediate on them this week, and be sure to thank God for all He is to you. He is the keeper of every promise.

Please pray with me, "Thank you, Lord, for every promise, that not one has ever failed. Thank you that I can apply them to my circumstances. Nothing is too hard for you, Lord, and I stand in awe of your capabilities. For you alone can see every promise through. You are the giver of life, and I owe you mine. Amen."

33
How Has He Changed Me?

Who comforts us in all our troubles so that we can comfort those in any trouble with the comfort we ourselves receive from God. 2 Corinthians 1:4

I'll never be the same. When I was going through my cancer treatment, I didn't see anything else happening except for the treatment. It seemed never-ending, and I couldn't even say the word cancer for a long time. It was like a foreign language. It was a community of people I didn't want to belong to. After coming out on the other side, I knew I would never be the same, but how had it changed me? I remembered the devotion I read the day I received my diagnosis.

"Are you ready to be poured out as an offering? It is an act of your will, not your emotions. Tell God without any complaints, despite what God may send your way. You must be willing to be placed on the altar and go through the fire; willing to experience what the altar represents – burning, purification, and separation for only one purpose – the elimination of every desire and affection not grounded in or directed toward God. But you don't eliminate it, God does. You 'bind the sacrifice…to the horns of the altar' and see to it that you don't wallow in self- pity once the fire begins. After you have gone through the fire, there will be nothing that will be able to trouble or depress you. When another crisis arises, you will realize that things cannot touch you as they used to do. Tell God you are ready to be poured out as an offering, and God will prove Himself to be all you ever dreamed He would be."

It's true, "He is all I've ever dreamed He would be."

God never gives us more than *He* can handle. There had come a point in my Christian walk where there was nowhere else to go. I knew He was sovereign and that He had never left me drowning in past trials. Still, it wasn't until I had gone through something of this magnitude that I saw Him orchestrating my every step. He was working everything together for my good and holding me safely in the palm of His skillful hand.

I had surrendered most things to Him by this point in my life, but I always held on to what I wanted to control. The root of that control I know now was fear. Once I realized I didn't have control over anything anyway, that He did and that He truly loved me, I fully surrendered everything to Him. It was a purposeful act that I remember doing. The complete resignation to His perfect will for my life transformed me.

Everything won't always work out the way we want it to because we are Christians, but God promises to work everything out for our good. We can count on that. We don't need to fear because He knows our future. It is a comfort to take every turn in the road with The One who holds that future.

We may not always understand or know why we are going through a trial. Still, we can always trust that God knows, and we can remind ourselves of His past faithfulness to us in previous tests.

Knowing He promises to work everything together for our good as Christians, we can rejoice in our suffering, whether we feel like it or not. God is using it to produce what we cannot produce in ourselves. If we walk through the trial with the Lord, we will be more Christ-like by the end of the test, and that is exciting!

As God sees you through trials in your life and you reflect on His faithfulness, it gets easier and easier to trust Him in the next one. He will never waste your hurt.

Think about how God has changed you through the trials in your life this week. How has he used them for your good? Make a list of the changes God has made in your life. What attitudes has He changed? What is He currently working on in you? What are you holding back from giving Him control over?

Read Hebrews 13:5 and look up the meaning of the word forsake. How do you know God will never leave you? Take a minute to thank God for His unwavering faithfulness.

Recently, I attended a one-day women's retreat. The speaker's testimony was a powerful one. She said her favorite words in the Bible are the verses that say, "*But God.*" I found 31 "*But God*" verses that I have listed below for your reference. This week, I challenge you to look up these verses for yourself. Those two words change everything.

The word "but" in the middle of a sentence nullifies everything before it. To put it another way, the words "*But God*" change everything that happened before them.

When God comes on the scene, He makes all things new. The song *See A Victory* says, "You take what the enemy meant for evil, and You turn it for good." Disease, circumstances, the enemy, and even death does not have the final say. There is always a "*But God.*"

Genesis 8:1
Genesis 31:7
Genesis 31:42
Genesis 31:23-24
Genesis 48:21
Genesis 50:20
Deuteronomy 7:7-8
1 Samuel 23:14
1 Kings 5:4
2 Chronicles 20:15
Psalm 49:14-15
Psalm 73:26
Psalm 86:15
Hosea 1:7
Jonah 2:6
Matthew 19:26

John1:18
Acts 2:24
Acts 3:15
Acts 7:9
Acts 10:28
Acts 13:29-30
Romans 5:8
Romans 6:23
I Corinthians 1:27
I Corinthians 2:10
I Corinthians 3:6
I Corinthians 10:13
Galatians 1:15-16
Galatians 3:18
II Timothy 2:9
Ephesians 2:1,3;4-5

34
What Would I Tell You?

I lift up my eyes to the mountains-where does my help come from? My help comes from the Lord, the Maker of heaven and earth. Psalm 121:1-2

But those who hope in the Lord will renew their strength. They will soar on wings like eagles; they will run and not grow weary, they will walk and not be faint. Isaiah 40:31

What would I tell someone who just got diagnosed with breast cancer, another unwanted diagnosis, or is facing a life-changing event?

I would tell them that no two stories are the same. If you have recently been diagnosed with breast cancer, you may not have to go through all the procedures I did, but if you do, God will be with you every step of the way. He never left me, and He has never forsaken me. His promises are true for every believing heart (see devotion 8).

I looked for someone exactly like me initially; HER2+, ER and PR-, Stage 2A, lymph node involvement, DMX with expanders, radiation, and reconstruction, but I never found anyone. We all have a different story, but we can all have the same hope in Jesus.

I'd tell them that God went before me and held my hand during every procedure. He gave me His strength when I didn't have any of my own, and there wasn't a need I had that He didn't meet

Himself or through another person. I'd assure them that God wants to do the same for them.

I'd tell them that I have no idea how; it is beyond my limited understanding, but, in God's miraculous way, life is better after going through a trial if you rely solely on the Lord to get you through it. I can't wrap my mind around that yet because I see some horrific scars when I look in the mirror, but somehow, I am happier now than before I had cancer. I try to think on a small part of the lyrics from *When We Fall Apart* by Ryan Stevenson:

You've got the gift of mercy
Don't ever think it's strange
Not a curse, but it is a blessing to feel other people's pain

Always love without condition
Trust the Lord with all your heart
There's healing in the story of your scars

The scars have somehow healed the unseen scars deep inside me that nothing else had ever been able to touch. They were there for so long; I didn't know how I had gotten them, *but God* heals from the inside out.

I'd tell them that a cancer diagnosis or any other unwanted diagnosis is an opportunity to surrender your whole being to God. We never really have control over anything anyway. I would tell them that the thing that was causing me so much pain and anguish in devotion number twenty-three no longer hurts me. It's not because I have realized it's a small thing in the big picture of life and death, because it is still a significant thing to me. But it no longer has the power to cut me deep, and I do not have any resentment or hard feelings associated with it.

I'd let them know that I felt embarrassed when I was first diagnosed with cancer. I would tell them they don't have anything to be embarrassed about and that it's not their fault. That was an important thing for me to hear, and I want them to know that too.

I would tell them to find support through the people that love them, and that they know will pray for them. Accept the meals and the flowers. Hold on to the cards. Reread them after you finish your treatment.

I would encourage them to see a comparison in what God does with our broken areas and the Japanese art of Kintsugi. Kintsugi is also referred to as the golden repair. It is the art of repairing broken pottery by taking the pieces and putting them back together with powdered gold. Like us, the pottery is made stronger by the process, each piece is made perfectly and beautifully unique, and its imperfections are embraced. He makes our flaws usable. When I look in the mirror, I can’t help but see my scars, but in them I see the masterpiece God is working in me. I have learned to embrace my brokenness.

You will not be the same after cancer. You will be better. Live every day because it's all any of us have anyway.

Get up every time you can and be thankful. This too shall pass.

What would I tell someone who just got diagnosed with breast cancer, another unwanted diagnosis, or is facing a life-changing event? Trust Him. He is worthy!

Please share my story with anyone you think it might help this week and start writing your testimony or personal story to share with others. It is a great way to minister to another person's heart.

35
Do You Trust Me?

Trust in the Lord with all your heart and lean not on your own understanding; in all your ways submit to him, and he will make your paths straight. Proverbs 3:5-6

In you, Lord my God, I put my *trust.* I *trust* in you; do not let me be put to shame, nor let my enemies triumph over me. Psalm 25:1-2

Commit your way to the Lord; trust in him and he will do this: He will make your righteous reward shine like the dawn, your vindication like the noonday sun. Psalm 37:5-6

A Godly, full-of-wisdom, skilled Christian counselor once told me a story of how the Lord led him to buy an orchard. After several years of struggling, he and his wife awoke to see the trees full of fruit like never before. They were ecstatic, but half of the fruit had died and fallen to the ground by the following day. He couldn't understand how the Lord would let this happen, which brought him to his knees in disappointment.

As he told me this story, he handed me a small red motorcycle with a cute silver kickstand that had stood on his desk for the entire three years I had been seeing him. "Once I give this to you," he said, "who does it belong to?" The answer was easy. It was mine. He said that is how it is with the Lord once we give something over to Him. The Lord asks us, "Do you really trust me with__________?" Then the counselor named the struggle I had been going through for the past three years.

He then shared that the fruit on his trees had died because the tree could not sustain all of it. It still ended up being a crop exceedingly more than he had ever expected!

That little red motorcycle now stands on my desk, and it constantly reminds me to ask myself, "Do I really trust you, Lord, in my current circumstance?"

Ask yourself today, "Do I really trust the Lord?" If not, ask the Lord to help you trust Him this week, and He will.

Keep a list of how you have shown the Lord you have trusted Him this week? Have you given Him a worry and not taken it back into your own hands? Have you trusted Him by acting on a prompting from the Holy Spirit or by living out a verse He has given you? Do you trust Him with everything?

There are so many pressures in life that God will free you from once you give them over to your Great Defender. Bask in His presence this week and enjoy every minute of it!

Part 3
Seeking God's Face

When you said, 'Seek my face,' my heart said to You, 'O LORD, I will seek Your face.'
Psalm 27:8

37
Abide In Me

I am the vine; you are the branches. If you remain in Me and I in you, you will bear much fruit; apart from Me you can do nothing. John 15:5

Every year I ask God for a word. It has been an incredible adventure! When He graciously gives me a word, I excitedly research it until I find a special meaning I can hold onto for the remainder of the year.

In 2013, He gave me the word deliverance, which means to rescue. In 2014, He gave me the word loss. I was grieving the loss of my dear mother that year. In 2015, He gave me the word healing, meaning to ease and to soften. In 2016, He gave me a word so late in the year I almost didn't think He was going to give me one. It was a powerful word. The word was revival, meaning comeback or advance. In 2017, He gave me the word resignation, meaning endurance and forbearance.

In December 2017, as I was looking forward to receiving my word from Him for 2018, I began reading 1 John out of my mom's Bible. This was the one she left me when she went to be with her Lord and Savior in 2013. I looked forward to reading it every morning. I never knew what treasure I might find inside. The treasure might be something she had underlined, one of her sidenotes, or a particular date she had written inside that reminded me of some family event. They were just about everywhere, and they each brought me peace and comfort as they were written in her familiar handwriting. On this morning, I saw where she had written, "great book." The words were written within the first few verses of chapter one, so I assumed she was referring to the book of 1 John.

I took my mom's Bible to work with me that day to show my coworker. I shared with her how I eagerly anticipate God's answer after asking Him for a word each year. As the two of us looked closer at my mom's Bible and the note she had written, we saw that it not only said, "great book," it said, "Abiding in Christ by Andrew Murray is a great book!" That's how I got the word abiding from the Lord for 2018. I immediately ordered the book, and it transformed my life!

As I read the book, I realized for the first time in my entire life that there is a deeper calling after receiving Jesus Christ into our hearts. The deeper calling is to abide *in* the Savior. **Our job is to set our minds on the things and thoughts of God, to surrender fully to Him, and to draw what we need from Him**. He is the Vine! We are the branches. God never intended for us to be the Vine. We are to rest in the Vine because, apart from Him, we can do nothing.

Once I consented to these truths, I put my complete trust in God. I understood He is the One to do the abiding for, in, and through me. It is God who keeps us and enables us to abide in Him. Once we set our minds on the things and thoughts of God and fully surrender to Him, we don't have to do anything through our own efforts. We can't and He knows that.

He came to give us an abundant life. The thief comes only to steal and kill and destroy; I have come that they may have life, and have it to the full. John 10:10

It's a failed and frustrating life when we try to live the Christian life in our own strength. We do not have to try to get God's approval, and we do not have to try to produce good works. When we abide in the Lord, day after day, our relationship with Him deepens, and doing His will becomes our deepest desire.

And with this new understanding, I was free from striving and able to rest in Him.

Ask yourself today, "Are you ready to be free?" Spend time with God every day this week and ask Him to bring the areas you have not yet surrendered to Him to your attention. Ask Him to help you fully surrender all that you are and have to Him, and He will.

In 2019, God gave me the word love, meaning to love them anyway. In 2020, he gave me the word willingness, meaning without complaint. In 2021, after being diagnosed with cancer, I completely forgot to ask God for a word. In 2022, after my chemotherapy and radiation treatments were completed, I felt disappointed in myself when I remembered I hadn't asked the Lord for a word in the last two years. As I sat in the morning service, my pastor gave all of us a very encouraging word for the new year and I was so happy to receive it. It was hope, meaning to live in expectation of something good. Are you living in expectation of something good? Where would you be today without hope?

Read Psalm 37.

Sweet Surrender

Abiding in Him
Surrendering all
I heard His voice
I answered His call.

As time wore on
I realized it then
There was much more
To surrender to Him.

With each anxiety
Or new fear I found
I bowed before Him
Knees to the ground.

It wasn't until
I had bowed many times
That I found His peace
The abiding kind.

It wasn't weakness
That made me give my worries away
It was the hardest thing
I've done to this day.

I must admit
There has not been one time
That He hasn't come through
On that worry of mine.

When something is troubling you
When dark turns the weather
Give it to God
Let Him cover you with His feather.

He will cover you with His feathers, and under His wings you will find refuge; His faithfulness will be your shield and rampart. Psalm 91:4

Ask yourself today, "Do you desire to nestle up under the protection of His wing?" Ask God to show you how to stop *striving* and start *abiding* this week. Find refuge in the One who does all the work.

Keep a list of what Abiding in Christ looks like to you this week. Invite Him into each day of the week and consider inviting Him in every day after. He desires a relationship with you, and there is a sweetness you will never know until He is a part of your daily life.

38
Learning to Sit Still and Abide

God Himself is the heart's desire of those who delight in Him.
Psalm 37:4 (Biblehub.com)

I have found that regular time spent fellowshipping with God in four ways helps me stay close to the Vine: reading His Word, spending time with Him in prayer, praising Him through worship, and connecting with Him and others through Christian service.

When I got out of the habit of reading my Bible regularly, and I was trying to get back on track, I started reading nine verses a day. I chose nine verses at the recommendation of Charles Stanley. He also suggests his listeners pray a short prayer before reading their Bibles, thanking God for giving them the desires of their heart, and asking Him to speak to them through His Word. It literally takes two minutes, and it was exciting when I began praying this prayer and reading my Bible every morning just how many little desires of my heart I started noticing He was fulfilling. After a while, my desire to read God's Word increased, and I stopped counting verses.

If you have gotten out of the habit of reading your Bible, start now by thanking God for giving you the desires of your heart and asking Him to speak to you through His Word. Then read nine verses and see how little time it takes. God's Word gives you wisdom, nourishment, joy, peace, hope, increased faith, a stronger relationship with your Savior, and strength for every battle. Reading the Bible is an absolute necessity for every Christian!

I choose to read my Bible first thing in the morning. I've found if I wait until later in the day, most of the time, it doesn't happen. But in some stages of our lives, there are little ones to feed and backpacks to get ready, and all of us can't always read our Bibles first thing in the morning. God understands.

Today, ask yourself, "What time during the day is the best time for me to commit to reading God's Word?" Ask Him to help you decide on that time and to protect it.

I found a special place in my home to be alone with God each morning. I got this idea from one of my Bible study leaders. She told our Bible study group how she would walk by the special place she had set aside in her home to be with the Lord several times every day and what a sweet reminder it was of the most precious time of her day. I chose a comfy couch by a lamp that I like in my front room to read my Bible by. On cold winter mornings, I grab a pretty throw and I burn a scented candle to make that dedicated time extra cozy.

Today, ask yourself, "Where would I like to meet with my Savior every day?" Ask God how He would like you to make the place you choose memorable for you and for Him.

So, with a cup of coffee in hand most mornings, a Bible in my lap every morning, and a pen and paper (you never know when you might want to write something down), I start my day.

A strong branch is filled with nourishment (God's Word) from the Vine. When I asked if you were ready to be strong at the beginning of this book, did you answer yes?

All scripture is God-breathed (2 Timothy 3:16), and there is tremendous power in it (Psalm 107:20). It is a lamp to our feet and a light to our path (Psalm 119:105). It is our nourishment (Matthew 4:4), our hope (Romans 15:4), and it endures forever (1 Peter 1:25). Scripture is alive (Hebrews 4:12), it defends, it protects (Ephesians 6:17), and it increases our faith (Romans 10:17). Let it direct your footsteps (Psalm 119:133).

What does your quiet time currently look like? How would you like it to look?

If you still don't think you need a regular quiet time with the Lord, or if you don't desire one, ask the Lord to change your heart, and He will. Consider making a commitment to the Lord to spend quality time with Him every day. Ask Him to help you figure out the best time and place so you can start abiding in Him.

Don't miss out on God's personal love letter to you!

39
The Importance of Prayer

Pray Continually, I Thessalonians 5:17

There have been times in my life when I have had a hard time praying. Sometimes I was in too much emotional or physical pain and I couldn't utter a word. Sometimes my prayer life became repetitious and I was bored. As much as I hate to admit it, there have been times I didn't think praying would make a difference. I was down and discouraged. I am here today to tell you that prayer makes all the difference!

I want to share what I have learned from anointed Bible study teachers, Christian podcasts, and God's Word that has brought excitement back to my prayer life. It has taught me to never stop praying because prayer changes everything!

- You are talking to the living God, and He delights in you. Don't ever forget whose presence you are *in* when you are praying.

- Knock and don't stop knocking. It's okay to keep coming to the Lord with the same prayer request.

- Pray until God gives you peace about your request or an answer.

- Don't forget how much God loves you. He wants a relationship with you. Nothing is too small to pray about. If it concerns you, it concerns Him. He is interested in the smallest detail of your life. He's a wonderful and caring God!

- Use a prayer journal to record your prayers and God's answers. Thank Him for the answers instead of asking Him for anything new occasionally. Share your answered prayer requests with others as encouragement. It's incredible to look back over your prayer journal and see all the prayer requests He has answered over the years. It can be interesting to see how your prayer requests have changed over the years too.

- If you feel your prayer requests are getting too monotonous, break them into groups and concentrate on those you have set aside to pray that day. You do not have to pray every prayer request every day. This one has been extremely helpful to me. Mixing your prayer requests up brings new life to them. Pray earnestly and wholeheartedly when you pray, making sure your requests are sincere and heartfelt.

- If you don't know what to pray for, ask the Holy Spirit to pray on your behalf, pray the Psalms, or sit still before the Lord in silence and allow Him to speak to you. Remember, tears are prayers too.

- Pray at the first sign of worry, anxiety, or any other negative emotion that threatens your peace. Nip your fret in the bud. Do not allow it to blossom.

- Pray for difficult people who cross your path during the day. Pray for people *before* you spend time with them. Ask for God's blessing on your time together and that your conversation be pleasing to Him. Ask for God to orchestrate your time together for His perfect will and pleasure. If everything doesn't go exactly as you had planned, thank God for making it exactly as He had planned.

- Talk to God throughout the day. He is always there, and you are never alone.

Take a few minutes and ask yourself, "When and where do I pray?" You may want to consider having a special place set aside in your home to be alone with the Lord and pray. It can be the same place where you have your daily devotions but remember God hears your prayers anytime and anywhere.

Ask God, "Who needs my prayers this week?" Ask a friend if there is anything you can be praying for them about.

The Room

Sitting quietly
Propped up in a chair
What on earth
Was she doing in there?

I'd seen her go in
A few times before
Entering quietly
Shutting the door

I wanted to follow
But somehow, I knew
It was for grown-ups
Must be something they do.

Abraham beget Isaac
She read from this book
My sister would giggle
Then came that look.

We read it through
From cover to cover
Through that warm summer
Next to our mother.

One day she took
Me to her side
It's time that you know
Where I go hide.

The Bible tells us
In Matthew Chapter 6
To go into a room
To pray in secret.

She took my hand
As I followed behind
Excited to share
In my mother's great find.

We entered the room
She shut the door
We knelt side by side
There on the floor.

I looked at her bowed
Starting to pray
I listened really close
What on earth would she say?

She thanked the Lord
For this little while
I nudged in real close
Catching her smile.

For I could tell
She was excited to be
Sharing that moment
Kneeling by me.

Thank you for our food
Our daily bread
For the clothes on our backs
A roof over our head.

She prayed for her friends
A neighbor to our right
She prayed for our safety
When out of her sight.

She prayed for her children
One after the other
The first time I witnessed
The love of a mother.

She gave us to God
Trusting in His ways
Asking Him to be with her
Throughout this day.

When she was done
I saw in her eye
A tear from heaven
As she started to cry.

I gave her a shirt sleeve
Having fallen to the floor
I learned a closet becomes a prayer room
Once you shut the door.

Is there anywhere in your home where you can pray in private? Consider your options this week.

Pray for the person or people God brings to your mind this week.

Add them to your prayer journal as a reminder to pray for them. Continue to add prayer requests and praises to your prayer journal throughout the week. Mix your prayers up daily to keep them fresh and new, so praying never becomes a mundane thing to do.

40
Turn on the *Worship* Music

Sing to the Lord a new song; sing to the Lord, all the earth. Sing to the Lord, praise His name; proclaim His salvation day after day. Psalm 96:1-2

I used to sing to hear myself. I grew up loving music, and I would often close my bedroom door and sing at the top of my lungs. Mostly I sang to albums as I daydreamed of what it would be like to sing on an actual stage.

When I was in my twenties, I started working part-time at a modeling agency. I helped the owner with classes in the evenings and an occasional fashion show on weekends. One year she decided to take a group of girls to New York City for the International Modeling and Talent Association convention, and I went.

Near the end of a line of over 850 singing hopefuls, I waited. I tried not to let my nerves get the best of me by chit-chatting with a few of the other contestants. Hours passed, the line got shorter, and finally, it was my turn to audition.

I chose a song by Sandi Patti, a popular Christian artist. I knew it was risky, but even at a young age, I took pride in my beliefs and being true to them. I prayed I wouldn't make a fool out of myself.

I didn't win first place, but I remember my surprise when I heard my name called to come up on stage with nine other contestants who had placed in the top ten. I thanked God with all my heart, finished my dinner listening to the first and second place winners sing "Greatest Love of All" by Whitney Houston, and was proud of my song selection.

It wasn't until years later, when I played contemporary Christian music in my own home, that I truly learned what singing worship music to the top of my lungs could really do; I no longer sang just to hear myself.

If it's music that you love too, ask yourself, "How can I use my love of music to glorify God this week?"

Has God blessed you with another talent or skill you can use to bless other people? Do you have the skills to fix someone's car this week or an appliance? Do you know how to set up a new TV or home computer? Can you change someone's oil? Do you have the means to give someone a ride to their doctor's appointment this week? We can offer a variety of talents and skills up to the Lord in service.

Consider calling your church office and finding out if there is a need in the church that you can meet this week. Don't go about your day until you have at least one concrete idea of how you can use a talent or skill God has given you to be a blessing to someone else this week. Write your idea down now and a description of how the person responded to your kindness after. How might you continue to bless others in the future?

41
Worship

Whenever the spirit from God came on Saul, David would take up his lyre and play. Then relief would come to Saul; he would feel better, and the evil spirit would leave him. 1 Samuel 16:23

I grew up in a home where country gospel music was played loudly and sung loudly by my mother. She had a record player that sat inside a big wooden cabinet in our living room with two large speakers in it. The record player played both 45s and 33s, but my mom mostly played albums. When I close my eyes, I can still hear her singing, and I can still recite some of the songs she sang word for word.

Living alone with two sons in a big house in a tiny town, I discovered the comfort of Christian radio. I soon found a favorite radio station, and I turned it on first thing every morning without fail. I left it on all day, and only turned it off right before getting in bed. It played through a small AM/FM transistor radio whether I was home or not during the day. I remember people asking me what was playing when they stopped by. Many times a song would come on the little radio, and the lyrics would seem divinely chosen for me as if God were speaking directly to my heart. These songs lifted my spirit.

Playing and singing worship music is powerful. It changes the atmosphere in your home, car, and church. It invites the Holy Spirit in. It calms emotions. The feeling it settled for me most often was anxiety, but worshiping God through music can alleviate all kinds of negative emotions, including fear and uncertainty. Paying attention to the lyrics we hear and sing can help our faith grow. It focuses our attention on God, taking the focus off ourselves.

If you haven't tried listening to Christian music, I encourage you to find a favorite style and a favorite radio station this week. See if K-Love or another Christian radio station that you like is available in your area. Leave it on in your house all day and play it in your car. Sing along, especially when you don't feel like it. Sing it at the top of your lungs! The effects of worshipping God are far-reaching.

I have a Christian playlist on Spotify called, "When a Heart Breaks" that you may find solace in and even a little humor. I created it as I was going through my cancer treatment. The songs will take you through my journey and inspire you to look to your heavenly Father no matter what you are going through.

42
The Giving Room

Each man should give what he has decided in his heart to give, not reluctantly or under compulsion, for God loves a cheerful giver. II Corinthians 9:7

I had read it takes between eighteen months and two years to make the successful transition from "mom" to "independent woman." Still, for almost five years I had been struggling with my empty nest. I had begun to wonder if I would ever get past it and be truly happy again.

Although my youngest son had returned home after serving five years in the air force and was now living in a small studio apartment in the back of our home, I had not re-purposed his room. Most of his things sat where he had left them.

Nothing about the room made me happy anymore. When I stared out from the bay window of his former bedroom, I could still picture him coming down the street from the bus stop and me anticipating that first glimpse. I could still hear the song he'd ask me to sing every night as I tucked him into bed. I could still hear the giggle he'd make when I blew on his tummy as I was getting ready to leave his room for the final time that night, and I could still remember identifying objects with him in a fiberoptic Christmas tree that sat in his bay window every Christmas. So the room sat.

When my son and I finally went through his room, I couldn't believe how many things I had been holding onto that didn't even work. I can't tell you how many times I held something up and he'd say, "That's broken." Of course, all of these items went directly into the trash. Once I took the trash out, and a few keepsake items had been boxed up and stored away, I surveyed the room and did what I had been doing for the last five years. I looked out the bay window remembering all the years I'd looked out of it. "What am I going to do with this room now?" I asked myself. I even googled, "What to do with an extra room?" but nothing fit. I already had a guest room and very few guests, a remarkable theatre room my husband had put together, and a treadmill in the garage that I used so no need for a designated workout room.

When the idea came to me, it didn't come to me in an extraordinary way. I was excitedly putting my testimony along with a pair of yellow socks in a gift bag when it dawned on me that this was my happy place. This room was where I made a care basket for my neighbor and assembled small gifts to take to the ladies at Bible study. Surprising someone with a little this or that brings me tremendous happiness. I love to encourage. I love to give. Giving is the love language I use to show others I care. And with that in mind the Giving Room was born.

I happily enter my son's old bedroom now. I have a gift wrapping, writing, craft-making table, and lots of storage for the little this and that's. Whenever I find an inexpensive gift box, a cute bag, or tissue paper, I put them neatly in the drawers of my son's old dresser. I also left my son's keyboard in the room so I can practice my newest undertaking. You will find me upstairs, filling the giving room with music when I don't want to bother anyone downstairs by practicing on the full-size piano.

What can you do for other people this week that brings you joy? Is it giving? Is it cooking a meal and taking it to a family who have lost a loved one, or who has a loved one who is recovering from surgery? Do you like to write notes or send cards to let others know you are thinking about them? Have you considered sponsoring a child and sending care packages to that child? Is it visiting others that brightens your day? It will also brighten theirs, a double blessing. The list of what you can do for others goes on and on. Don't stop until you figure out what you love to do for others.

If you can't think of anything offhand, ask God to bring people in need to your attention throughout the week and commit to doing at least one thing for another person. Consider making this a habit once a month or more as your schedule allows.

43
The Power of the Holy Spirit

The most beautiful way I have ever heard the power of the Holy Spirit described came from my pastor through this illustration.

Suppose you saw an artist with an easel set up on the sidewalk, and you loved what he was painting so you asked him how he did it. You went to the store and bought all the supplies he uses. You set up all your supplies right next to his. In that case, you could work all day alongside him, make every stroke he makes, but, at the end of the day, his painting would be a masterpiece and yours, at the very best, an imitation. The only way you could draw his painting is if he came inside of you to paint it. That's what the Holy Spirit does. He comes inside of us and works His masterpiece.

The minute you cry out to God with a sincere and repentant heart, He fills you with the Holy Spirit.

And you also were included in Christ when you heard the message of truth, the gospel of your salvation. When you believe, you were marked in him with a seal, the promised Holy Spirit, who is a deposit guaranteeing our inheritance until the redemption of those who are God's possession—to the praise of his glory. Ephesians 1:13-14

The Holy Spirit fills us (Ephesians 5:18), seals us (Ephesians 1:13), permanently lives in us (John 14:16-17), equips us (I Corinthians 12:4-7), reminds us (John 14:26), directs our prayers (Romans 8:27), leads us (John 16:13), empowers us (Acts 1:8), and bears fruit through us (Galatians 5:22-23). He is our Helper, our Strength, and our Power.

Read Ephesians 6:12. Spiritual warfare is real, and God's Word is a sword to the Holy Spirit to fight off the enemy when we are under attack. Who wants to be caught without their sword?

Ask God right now for whatever discipline you need to make time to put His Word in your heart daily. And if you have asked Jesus into your heart, ask Him to give you a fresh filling of the Holy Spirit whenever you need it throughout the week.

44
Decluttering

To everything there is a season…a time to keep and a time to cast away.
Ecclesiastes 3:6

When my boys were seven and four and a half, my husband left us for the third time. I will never forget when he sat down on the couch next to me and told me he didn't love me anymore. I still loved him very much, and I was devastated. He moved out the next day. At first, and for a short time, he saw the boys regularly. But every other weekend soon turned into every other Saturday.

My heart hurt for them. My husband filed for divorce, and he moved away. But he continued to take me to court. He took me to court for four years. He took me to court because the kid's shoes were too small, so I bought some bigger ones. Then he took me to court because the kid's shoes were too big. I wish I were kidding. As his behavior escalated, I had to get a restraining order. I was parent and protector. My boys and I grew very close during this time. Every decision I made was for them. I was walking closely with the Lord before my husband left me, and second to God, my boys were my passion. My court file had gained much attention as it quickly spread across an entire bookcase in my attorney's office.

Right now, you are probably wondering what this has to do with decluttering. Well, I had duplicate copies of all those court documents at home, an entire bookcase full.

So fast forward twenty years, and my "passions" are moving out. My youngest son leaves first unexpectantly. He decides to join the U.S. Air Force as a Photojournalist. He tells me it's going to be like jumping in the pool. At first, he will hate it, but he will adjust. My oldest son falls in love, proposes, and starts planning a wedding.

I'm proud of my boys. I raised them to be independent and they are. They have overcome significant obstacles, and they are excelling. I am genuinely excited for them, and I am still busy with a full-time job, a husband, and a few great friends. But suddenly, my life feels empty.

At this time, I went over to my friend Annie's house to catch up. We had traveled to Israel together years earlier with Calvary Chapel Church. She had just had surgery, and I wanted to see how she was doing. As we were sharing, I told her how I'd been praying for a new passion, something with purpose that would bring excitement into my life again. She recommended a book on decluttering. That wasn't exactly what I had in mind I told her and laughed. She told me the book was on the New York Bestseller's list. The book's title was "The Life- Changing Magic of Tidying Up" by Marie Kondo.

It was funny because it was on People Magazine's cover when I went to the store on my way home.

Two days later, it arrived in my mailbox, courtesy of Annie. I started reading it and began passionately cleaning.

I learned that when you begin to declutter, it is essential to go through categories in a specific order, and not room by room. It's also vital that you put every item (from every room and closet) from the category you are working on in an open area where you can see them and not shut a door to get away from them.

For example, start with your tops. Put everything you wear from the waist up in a pile. Do not try the tops on. Simply look at them and feel them. Do they bring you joy? If not, discard them. Do not keep anything that is torn or stained. It's important that you feel good in your clothing. This can boost your confidence. Consider cutting up your torn clothing and using it for dish rags, donating it to a center that sells the fabric by the pound to rag-makers, or donating it to dog shelters for dog bedding. Try to finish going through all your tops in one afternoon, or day, and try to finish the entire decluttering project within six months.

I want to share with you what I learned through the process of decluttering:

- Once I got rid of stuff, I no longer had a purpose for, I could truly appreciate the things I do have.

- The things I got rid of brought happiness to other people, bringing me much more joy than having them.

- It's okay to get rid of a gift someone gave me if I don't like it or, have a purpose for it. The gift is in the thought and the giving.

- If I didn't make tidying up a one-time event, tidy up by categories, and continued to tidy up room by room, I do think I would be tidying up forever!

- As I freed myself from unnecessary clutter, I had more time for Him.

- I had enough storage space. Neatly folding most of my clothes solved all my storage problems.

- The more I decluttered, the more I looked forward to it. It felt good, it was satisfying, and it was fun! I enjoyed it so much I started teaching a class on it!

- I learned to live in the present.

- My space feels calmer.

- I learned that clutter can be a self-control issue. We live in a world where more and bigger is better. The truth is the tiniest garden is often the loveliest.

- Once I had finished decluttering, I realized I had learned only to buy unique things that I love. I no longer buy stuff I "like" or simply because it is on sale.

If you have thought about decluttering before, it's time to do it!

Six months after decluttering, I was able to confidently say:

- Getting dressed is no longer a chore. I know what I have and where everything is.

- The actual holes in my wardrobe have been identified.

- I love what I am collecting.

- Everything has a place, and the effort to put things away has diminished.

- Cleaning is so much easier!

When I finished decluttering, I donated 35 large black trash bags full of "stuff!"

I like how Jim Elliot puts it, "Let's let go of what we can't keep anyhow, and cling to what we can never lose!"

What do you have an excess of that you can give to others?

Anyone who has two shirts should share with the one who has none; and anyone who has food should do the same. Luke 3:11

Take some time putting your excess items together this week, and donate them to someone in need.

Thank God for the opportunity to give from the abundance He has given you. Thank Him that the relationship you have with Him is everlasting, and He is ours forever. He is the only thing we should ever cling to.

Do not store up for yourselves treasures on earth, where moth and vermin destroy, and where thieves break in and steal. But store up for yourselves treasures in heaven, where moth and vermin do not destroy, and where thieves do not break in and steal. Matthew 6:19-20

45
Spiritual Decluttering

The tiniest garden is often the loveliest – Vita Sackville West.

This quote was written on my dining room wall for 19 years.

In 2017, I started teaching a class on decluttering. I googled the word "stuff" and was sickened by the meanings. Stuff as a noun is described as matter, material, articles, personal belongings, worthless things, dated and worthless ideas, and inward character, qualities, or capabilities. Examples given were: What's all this stuff on my desk? and I think he has the right stuff for the job. As a verb, stuff is described as filling completely, cramming full, forcing, shoving, squeezing, filling, to cram with food, gorge, clutter, stop up, plug, block, or choke. The British informal synonym is to defeat utterly, or win a resounding victory over.

I enjoy teaching the class, but even more so, I enjoy being invited over to the homes of my class participants to help them start the decluttering process. Some visits have gone better than others. At one of these homes, I realized an even more critical step in the decluttering process, spiritual decluttering. Through my own decluttering experience, I realize what an emotional experience decluttering can be, and some people are not ready for that. Remember my divorce papers? As I went through them page by page, I relived the whole process, but it also helped me work through the grief.

The items in our closets and our home reveal a lot about us. They show what's important to us and, in some cases, what we haven't been able to let go of. Our minds, hearts, and physical possessions are linked.

One of the spiritual lessons I learned when I was decluttering was how easy it is to get stuck in the past. No matter how much we miss the way our lives were, we mustn't allow ourselves to get stuck there. We need to live each moment God gives us to the fullest. They are a gift, and they will never come again.

Things that remind us of yesterday are the hardest to let go of, and that is why they are the last items you go through in the decluttering process. By the time you get to them, you will have learned how to identify what really brings you joy, and letting go will have become easier.

We tend to hold onto a loved one's "stuff" when we are grieving their loss. This can serve as an essential part of the grieving process for a while. Still, we never really allow ourselves to have closure in holding onto their belongings forever.

When you are ready, and not until then, go through your loved one's things. Please don't make the mistake of putting boxes and boxes under your bed or in a storage shed to be gone through later. I can't tell you how many people have told me they have done precisely that, and ten or twenty years later, the items are still there. They keep thinking that they need to go through them, which has become a source of stress for the individual.

Instead, go through the boxes and keep the items you will genuinely treasure. Pass down what you want to and display what you have decided to keep in your loved one's memory.

When we thoroughly declutter, this includes our hearts. Once we clear things away, there is a space for "the you" Christ has called according to His purpose.

Make space for time with Him each morning, if possible. It begins your fellowship with the Lord that lasts all day. Read your Bible until you find at least one "gold nugget," a word of truth or wisdom, to hold onto for the rest of the day. Reading scripture gives the Holy Spirit something to bring to our memory when we need it most. The more we know of His Word, the more we know of His will. Scripture reveals who we are in Christ. What it reveals it can heal, not only physical healing but also emotional healing. He wants to declutter every area of our lives so we can fully enjoy the freedom He has come to bless us with.

Once we have decluttered, we won't have to clean, shop, or maintain what we have as often because we won't have as much. We will have time for what is essential, like saving lives, quality time with God and loved ones, concentrating on God's call for our lives, impacting others, date nights, visiting friends, or playing with our kids and pets. God knows what spiritual opportunities will make us the happiest. These types of things are of so much more value than anything material.

Chaos is stressful, whether it is a cluttered space in our home or an overwhelmed schedule. Creating more physical and material space creates more emotional freedom. Matthew 19 tells us about a man who has kept all of God's commandments, and when he asks Jesus what he lacks, Jesus tells him to go home and sell his "stuff," give it to the poor and follow Me. The rich man walks away sad because he has many "things." His "stuff" stopped him from following Jesus. Is your "stuff" stopping you from following Jesus?

Jesus trusted God to meet all His needs. Do you?

More questions to ponder this week:

- Does your "stuff" give you false security?
- Does your "stuff" take hours to sort through and organize each month?
- Are you devouring hours and hours with the upkeep of your "stuff?"

- Do you buy things at the store because you're unsure if you have them at home, or you know you have them but you can't find them?

- Do you have enough "stuff" but you want to keep shopping?

- Do you have more clothes than you can wear?

- Why do our hearts cling to "stuff" that we can't take with us?

It may surprise you that once you have decluttered and removed those items you don't love from your house, you won't miss them.

Focus on the area of spiritual decluttering this week. Pray and ask God to bring any issues He sees in your life concerning this area to your mind. Ask God to shine His light on what is getting in your way of "living life." Ask God to help you make a list of the "stuff" that is of the most significant importance to you this week, and don't be surprised if the list is short.

Consider putting down your "stuff" and following Him.

46
Decluttering, the Poem

Be still, and know that I am God. Psalm 46:10

Simply

Over the years
We'd had lots of fun
Leaving boring tasks
Simply undone.

Making time for bedtime stories
Always some prayer
A sock or a toy
Just stick it somewhere.

Blowing on his tummy
Brushing his hair
Much left undone
But I didn't care.

Eyes barely open
I need to rest
Oh, that little thing
I think there's room in the chest.

Running in and out
Just one more hug
A handmade gift for me?
He says, "I made it with love!"

Christmas morning
The pitter patter of tiny feet
Suddenly my new house
Wasn't that neat.

Company is coming over?
Is that what he said?
Hurry up kids
Put that under the bed.

Is there room in that closet?
A little to the right
I'll move it tomorrow
Kids, please don't fight.

Dinner and homework
As we rushed about
Quick, time for a tickle
An expected gleeful shout.

Put it in that basket
The one by the door
Time to sell cookies
It's already 4:00.

Don't forget your homework
We worked on it all night
Over by the phone
Time for a quick bite?

Go grab your backpack
You'll miss the bus
Just put it in that pile
No time to fuss.

Plenty of sleepovers
Video games
That neat tidy house
Forever then changed!

The pitter patter of feet
Became larger indeed
As little boys turned into teenagers
For me, there was less need.

Run to the bank
Withdrawal the deposit
Arms full of groceries
I'll just stick this one last thing right in that closet!

Walking the dog alone
Fewer cookies to make
Times started changing
My heart felt an ache.

Grab some cereal son
I've got to run
I'm a bankruptcy clerk
Where everything must be done!

The youngest left first
To defend our country
A photojournalist with the Air Force
Was what he would be.

One day it got quiet
On my heartstrings, one last tug
"I'm going to go marry
the one that I love."

They were soon grown
I was so proud
But my house was so quiet
And the mess was so loud!

There's magic in tidying up?
Is that what I read?
I put the book down
Looked under my bed!

I looked in places
I hadn't for years
I went through old papers
I cried a few tears.

As my space started to take shape
My new passion for cleanliness pressed on
Until each page was read
And each task had been done.

When you put things away
Use your time wisely and smart
Make your house a little tidier
Do a full declutter of your heart.

I walk into my house today
There's joy everywhere
Time for the important stuff
Which is most definitely prayer.

There isn't a day
That doesn't go by
I don't think of my little boys
And how simply time flies.

The clutter is quiet now
Time to make some new fun
Time for tea in my favorite cup
Because it's all simply done.

The Lord's voice is heard softly now
My heart fully decluttered
"Job well done, my good and faithful servant.
You were a terrific mother!"

When my boys grew up and moved away, I felt like I'd lost my purpose. It was a difficult time for me, and it took me a long time to realize I will always be their mom. But being a mom is not my only purpose. I am free to find the life-changing magic of my purpose in God.

Spiritual decluttering is not all about what we should discard. It's important to remember what we should "keep." We should keep our eyes fixed on the Lord and keep our Bibles close and open.

Consider starting the decluttering process this week. Is there anything holding you back from getting started? What are some of the benefits you may experience once you start? Ask the Lord to help you let go of the unnecessary clutter in your life and to help you identify anything taking the place in your life that He deserves to fill. What does letting go mean to you? What do you think letting go means to God?

47
Spiritual Gifts

There are different kinds of gifts, but the same spirit distributes them.
I Corinthians 12:4

I believe spiritual gifts are for today and that each Christian receives at least one spiritual gift. I always thought mine was the Gift of Exhortation until I sat through a teaching on spiritual gifts. The illustration given in the teaching went something like this:

You are at a friend's house, and she has a four-year- old daughter. You are already seated along with other guests when the little girl comes into the room wearing a beautiful cream-colored dress. She is carrying a tray that holds a glass pitcher of pink lemonade and crystal goblets. The room you are sitting in is exquisitely decorated, including a lovely, thick area rug covering the carpet. You notice the tile floor next to the rug when, suddenly, you see the little girl trip over the thick rug, and everything on the tray comes crashing to the ground. The pitcher and the goblets are broken, and the carpet and the little girl are covered in pink lemonade. The little girl starts to cry.

Your initial response to this illustration may help you identify your spiritual gift(s).

If you are gifted in the Word of Knowledge, you may react to the little girl by saying something like, "You were looking for your apron, and you were so upset when you couldn't find it you weren't paying attention when you tripped. But don't worry because your dress is not going to stain."

If you have the Gift of Prophesy, you may respond by saying, "You fell, but our God is the God of second chances, and He wants you to get up and try again. You will do better next time."

Those with the Gift of Helps may say, "Let me help you. Let me clean this all up and dust you off."

Someone with the Gift of Teaching may say, "Let me show you how to carry that tray. It has two handles, and you hold onto them like this."

If the Gift of Exhortation is your spiritual gift, you may say, "Don't give up! Come on! Get in there. Do it again. You can do it!" This was not me.

An individual with the Gift of Leadership immediately starts assigning tasks. "You aren't helping over here. You need to go over there and you," pointing to someone else, "need to get the dustpan." The leader may even move the carpet out.

The Gift of Mercy sees nothing but the little girl and her heart. This person is kneeling in broken glass, consoling the little girl. This was me!

A person with the Gift of Giving may say, "I know you don't have the money to pay for this. I will pay for it, and I will buy you a new dress!"

Jokingly the illustration ends with the Christian who has the Gift of Miracles rewinding the whole situation back to the beginning. The rug has been moved, and no one ever trips.

What would your first response be to the situation?

Before the lesson was over, I knew which gift I had. I hope you do too. As soon as the little girl tripped, my heart went out to her, and I wanted to make sure she was okay. The room became secondary.

Months after this teaching, a lingering trial brought me to my knees before God. I just wanted it to be over. My thoughts were tormenting me, and I hadn't been sleeping well. I felt left out by someone I longed to be close to. I was literally at my wit's end when I pleaded with the Lord, who I knew held the key to my sadness, "I need to understand why this is breaking my heart," I said as I begged Him for an answer. "I'm doing everything I know to do. I'm reading your word. I'm praying. I'm praising you even when I don't feel like it, and nothing is changing. Even if the situation stays the same, please take the pain associated with it away."

I felt resigned to carry this burden with me for the rest of the day, but when I turned on my car radio, I was met by a familiar voice. It was Charles Stanley speaking from my favorite radio station.

I had been attentively waiting as he had been discussing each spiritual gift separately this week, eagerly waiting to hear about mine. The broadcast was almost over, but as I pulled out of my driveway, I heard what God wanted me to hear.

"The people with this gift close their spirits off to insensitive people. They simply can't handle it. They get hurt more than any other spiritual gift." What!? Could my spiritual gift be the cause of my pain? The gift he was speaking of was the gift of mercy, and it was mine. It was one of the quickest answers I have ever received from the Lord. I still didn't know what to do differently in the trial I was in, but I understood myself in a way I never had before. I even appreciated my younger self better. I learned later that I was doing what we all should do in a trial; bow down, pray, praise God through worship whether we feel like it or not, read His Word, and sit still.

Read I Corinthians 12:4-7 and verse 11 in the New Living Translation, if possible. What spiritual gift(s) do you have? If you are unsure, spend time with the Lord this week and ask Him to help you identify the gift(s) He has given especially to you, His unique and deeply loved son or daughter.

48
For Raising Them with Me – A Note of Thanksgiving

I thank my God upon every remembrance of you. Philippians 1:3

Below is a note I wrote to my husband, my boy's bonus dad, one Father's Day.

Thank you for every back-to-school night you went to with me, every karate tournament you attended, and every basketball you threw or tried to throw through the hoop in our cul-de-sac. Thank you for the missions and pinewood derby cars you spent hours helping to build, for picking up the boy's first puppy at the airport, and for helping me decide when the boys needed stitches. Thank you for all the trips you made to the dentist, the doctor, the vet, and for every prescription you picked up. Thank you for every meal you cooked us, for helping me decide if the boys should be allowed to go, what time they should be home, and if they should be hanging around that friend or not. Thank you for encouraging me through all the homework, for taking us to church on Sundays, for all the Christmas shopping trips we took looking for the most popular toy that year, and for all the broken toys you fixed after. Thank you for helping the boys get their first cars and teaching them how to take care of them. Thank you for caring that they make something out of their lives. That is a dad, and my boys had a wonderful one because of you. Happy Father's Day.

And now I can add…Thank you for keeping your wedding vow to me, "In sickness and in health," and for faithfully giving me 30 shots during my cancer treatment.

Is there anyone who chose to be there for you, or for someone important to you when it wasn't their responsibility? Did you have a bonus parent who tried to keep you on the right path, a teacher, a friend, or a pastor who cared? Has God used someone else to meet your needs? If so, write them a note of thanksgiving this week.

49
When my dad met Jesus

"On one of these journeys I was going to Damascus with the authority and commission of the chief priests. About noon, King Agrippa, as I was on the road, I saw a light from heaven, brighter than the sun, blazing around me and my companions. We all fell to the ground, and I heard a voice saying to me in Aramaic, 'Saul, Saul, why do you persecute me? It is hard for you to kick against the goads.' "Then I asked, 'Who are you, Lord?' "'I am Jesus, whom you are persecuting,' the Lord replied. 'Now get up and stand on your feet. I have appeared to you to appoint you as a servant and as a witness of what you have seen and will see of me. I will rescue you from your own people and from the Gentiles. I am sending you to them to open their eyes and turn them from darkness to light, and from the power of Satan to God, so that they may receive forgiveness of sins and a place among those who are sanctified by faith in me.' Acts 26:12-18

Apostle Paul persecuted the early disciples of Jesus before he became a Christian. He is an example of a man that no one ever thought would come to know the Lord.

We had barely sat down in the hospital cafeteria when we were summoned over the loudspeaker, "The Hilligoss family, please return to ICU … Hilligoss family needed in ICU." After hours of sitting by our dad's side, we had finally convinced our mother to grab a bite to eat with us in the downstairs cafeteria. Leaving our trays behind, we frantically rushed back upstairs, but it was too late. Our dad was gone.

My mom went to church as a young girl, but neither my father nor mother were Christians when they got married. My mom became a Christian at forty-four years of age after some Christian women came to her door for Bible study. This was the beginning of a Bible study group she participated in for 40 years with her best friend Rita. You may remember her from an earlier devotion.

We never attended church as a family, but I do remember my dad taking me to one service at a church his friend attended. My dad asked me if I would like to sing there. My dad and I didn't go back but I got a ride to the Baptist church my sister and brother were going to from another high school student and I went every week after. My brother received Christ at one of the high school church camps where he also met his wife. I know my dad had heard about the Lord many times over his lifetime. My brother, sister, and mother had all shared with him. Still, he would never make the decision to follow Jesus on his own.

He seemed so small to me as he lay there in the hospital bed. He wasn't nearly as big as I had remembered him. His deep, coarse voice would make you picture a much larger man if that was all you had to go on. Our mother often told us what a hard worker and good provider our father was, but none of us would have described him as a Godly man.

When you tell someone you love about the Lord over and over again, hoping they will see by the way you live your life that the Lord is real and true, and they continually reject Him, it is easy to give up hope that they will ever come to know the Lord as their personal Savior. It's easy to get discouraged and stop praying for that person altogether. When I am guilty of putting someone in the "never" category, I think of Jesus and the apostle Paul. Jesus's own brothers didn't believe Him, and Paul was the last person anyone ever thought would be saved. Acts 9:1-22 shows us that no one is hopeless and we should never put anyone in the "never" category.

It wasn't until the very end of my dad's life, as he lay dying in a hospital bed, that he prayed with my brother and asked Jesus into his life. I'm so glad my dad didn't get put in the "never" category.

Although my dad died way too young, at the age of sixty-four, and I was sad that my life with him had not been all I had hoped it would be, our whole family knew that we would see him again, and knowing that brought us great comfort.

Read Acts 9:1-22 and Acts 22:6-21.

Is there anyone you have put in the "never" category? Pray for them now and throughout the coming week. Commit them to God's hands and continue to pray for them until they come to know the Lord. No one is hopeless.

50
In the Garden

Early on the first day of the week, while it was still dark, Mary Magdalene went to the tomb and saw that the stone had been removed from the entrance. So she came running to Simon Peter and the other disciple, the one Jesus loved, and said, "They have taken the Lord out of the tomb, and we don't know where they have put him!" So Peter and the other disciple started for the tomb. Both were running, but the other disciple outran Peter and reached the tomb first. He bent over and looked in at the strips of linen lying there but did not go in.Then Simon Peter came along behind him and went straight into the tomb. He saw the strips of linen lying there, as well as the cloth that had been wrapped around Jesus' head. The cloth was still lying in its place, separate from the linen. Finally the other disciple, who had reached the tomb first, also went inside. He saw and believed. (They still did not understand from Scripture that Jesus had to rise from the dead.) Then the disciples went back to where they were staying. Now Mary stood outside the tomb crying. As she wept, she bent over to look into the tomb and saw two angels in white, seated where Jesus' body had been, one at the head and the other at the foot. They asked her, "Woman, why are you crying?" "They have taken my Lord away," she said, "and I don't know where they have put him." At this, she turned around and saw Jesus standing there, but she did not realize that it was Jesus. He asked her, "Woman, why are you crying? Who is it you are looking for?" Thinking he was the gardener, she said, "Sir, if you have carried him away, tell me where you have put him, and I will get him." Jesus said to her, "Mary." She turned toward him and cried out in Aramaic, "Rabboni!" (which means "Teacher"). Jesus said, "Do not hold on to me, for I have not yet ascended to the Father. Go instead to my brothers and tell them, 'I am ascending to my Father and your Father, to my God and your God.'" Mary Magdalene went to the disciples with the news: "I have seen the Lord!" And she told them that he had said these things to her. John Chapter 20: 1- 18

My dad's favorite hymn was "In the Garden" by C. Austin Miles. Written in 1912, these lyrics are the story of what happened between Mary Magdalene and Jesus not long after Jesus's resurrection.

I come to the garden alone,
While the dew is still on the roses,
And the voice I hear falling on my ear,
The Son of God Discloses…

And He walks with me, and He talks with me,
And He tells me I am His own,
And the joy we share as we tarry there,
None other, has ever, known!

He speaks and the sound of His voice,
Is so sweet the birds hush their singing,
And the melody that He gave to me,
Within my heart is ringing…

And He walks with me, and He talks with me,
And He tells me I am His own,
And the joy we share as we tarry there,
None other, has ever, known!

And the joy we share as we tarry there,
None other, has ever, known!

Thank you, Lord, that my dad is with you for eternity. Thank you that He didn't die without knowing you. Thank you for meeting Him in the garden of heaven, for walking and talking with Him. Thank you for making him Your own.

Take some time each day this week to pray for your unbelieving loved ones. Also thank the Lord for any of your Christian loved ones that He has met at the end of their lives and has taken them home to be with Him.

51
Come To Me

For God so loved the world that He gave His one and only Son, that whoever believes in Him shall not perish but have eternal life. John 3:16

Charles Stanley, the founder of In Touch Ministries and Pastor Emeritus of the First Baptist Church of Atlanta, Georgia for more than 50 years, encourages his listeners to write this definition down and to share it with others:

"*To believe in Jesus* is to have a confident conviction that He is who the Bible says He is, He will keep His promises, and upon placing your trust in Him, you are entering into a personal, eternal relationship with the Son of God."

Do you believe it?

This devotion is repeated. You read it on day seven. It is repeated for a reason that I can not stress enough. "Do you believe it?" is the most important question you will ever answer. Your very life and afterlife depend on the answer.

Have you placed your trust in Jesus Christ? If you have, congratulations! If not, is He calling you to begin a relationship with Him today?

If your answer is yes, all you have to do is pray this prayer and mean it with your whole heart:

Lord Jesus,

As You stand at the door and knock, I open my heart to You. I realize I am less than perfect (a sinner). I ask You to forgive me of my sins. I believe You sent Your only Son Jesus to die in my place for my sins. Make me who I am supposed to be in Jesus Christ. I thank You for coming into my life and for saving me. In Jesus' name. Amen.

"Behold, I stand at the door and knock. If anyone hears My voice and opens the door, I will come in…" Revelation 3:20

I am living today to tell you that you can trust His promises.

If you have prayed this prayer, tell someone this week. If you haven't connected with a home church, look for one. Start spending time alone in prayer, praise, and His Word. Consider starting this devotional book over as a Christian and ask God to speak to you through it, and He will.

If you answered yes to the question, "Do you believe?" have you considered being baptized in the Holy Spirit? The Baptism in the Holy Spirit is a separate and distinct experience to that of giving your life to Christ and trusting Him for your salvation. It occurs either after or simultaneous at the time of salvation. It is evidenced in a Christian's life by giving it a greater dynamic, enabling that person to be a more effective witness and a bolder one. The supreme evidence of the infilling of the Holy Spirit in a person's life is love, which is one of the Fruits of the Spirit. (Galatians 5:22-23) The Holy Spirit indwells every believer in Jesus Christ, and He is every Christian's abiding teacher, helper, and guide. (John 14:16-17, 16:8-11,13; Acts 1:8; Romans 8:26, 15:13,16; II Corinthians 3:18; Hebrews 9:14).

52
Robert

He loved a jug of iced tea
At the end of the day
"I can't complain"
He'd often say.

He loved clam chowder
Fishing, reading true crime
Worked hard for his family
As we counted each dime.

He liked *All in the Family*
Sanford and Son
Saltine and Cheez-it crackers
And every rerun.

He worked as a sheriff
Police officer too
He smoked back in the day
When smoking was cool.

He owned a two-door green truck
I'd climb in the back
We'd drive to Round Table for a cheese pizza
He had a brother named Jack.

When we moved into our house
He put in the yards
Always gave us a little money
For a good report card.

He was a hard worker
Mom told us so
He always kept his word
She wanted us to know.

He liked sitting by the campfire
Mount Madonna, Lyons Lake
The boardwalk at Santa Cruz
He was up at daybreak.

He liked watching TV
His favorite team
The 49ers
On our 25-inch screen.

My mom gave him a 49er jacket
He went back to buy her a doll
Fond memories because I knew
Our income was small.

He often wore a green sweater
It hung on the back of his chair
The same chair I ran around on the oval rug
As he'd say, "Can you go light somewhere?"

He drove my brother to Sea Cadet training
A tiny purple ring bought on the way
I felt very special wearing it
I still have it to this day.

Just the two of us sitting
In a caboose eating Italian food
I ate the huge olive out of his beer
On his forearm my mom's name tattooed.

He liked medieval décor
Making model planes
Flying them with my brother
And building towns with trains.

His love for his dog Charlie
Cannot be understated
Fall was his favorite season
Painting he truly hated.

He answered our questions
"Are we there yet?"
He taught us many things
We'd never forget.

The importance of working hard
Dependability
To be loyal and be honest
Life's fragility.

Much more than he had
He tried to give all us kids
Make our Christmases merry
He loved all his grandkids.

A few times I saw him dancing
In the kitchen with my mom
Waltzing about sillily
Holding her in his arms.

A protector of his family
God heard his cries
When he asked Him to take
Not mine but his eyes.

Proud of his chicken seasoning
He cooked with it often
And as he grew older
I think his heart started to soften.

So, when he laid there
Preparing to die
Listening to my brother's testimony
He prayed to the Lord most high.

He's now in heaven
My mother the same
I'm proud of my father
All he overcame.

When I think about him now
I think about the good
None of us are perfect this side of heaven
But he did the best he could.

Thank you for always doing the best you could, Dad.

Today I live with my husband, John, and two Shih Tzus, Aslan and Koda. I am cancer-free and went on the Footsteps of Paul trip initially scheduled for March 2020 in May 2022. With all the travel delays due to Covid-19, the woman I gave my trip to decided to go to Israel in March of 2022 instead. She had a wonderful time and said she would never have gone had it not been for me first giving her the Footsteps of Paul trip.

In March 2020, I walked into the high school room at church to pick up my information packet for the Footsteps of Paul trip, knowing I wasn't going. No one else knew I had been diagnosed with an aggressive form of breast cancer, and I needed to start treatment immediately. I felt the excitement in the room as everyone's name was called to go up to the front of the room and collect their packets. I was embraced by people, "Oh, I'm so excited you are going on the trip with us!" I accepted their hugs, unable to get out of the room fast enough. My disappointment was starting to brim over my lower eyelashes and onto my cheeks.

In April of 2022, I walked into the same room for the same reason, to claim my instruction packet for the Footsteps of Paul trip. But this time, the tears were tears of joy. How could this be? It was truly unbelievable, and I could barely wrap my mind around it. This time I was going on the same trip, only two years later. I remembered Job 2:25. God restored everything to me that the enemy had stolen.

www.ingramcontent.com/pod-product-compliance
Ingram Content Group UK Ltd.
Pitfield, Milton Keynes, MK11 3LW, UK
UKHW062256290726
14090UKWH00017B/734

9 798218 034047